ABUNDANCE
LEADERS

LAURA FREEBAIRN-SMITH

ABUNDANCE
LEADERS

CREATING

ENERGY, JOY, AND **PRODUCTIVITY**

IN AN **UNSETTLED WORLD**

WILEY

Published by John Wiley & Sons, Inc., Hoboken, New Jersey.
Published simultaneously in Canada.

For general information on our other products and services or for technical support, please contact our Customer Care Department within the United States at (800) 762-2974, outside the United States at (317) 572-3993 or fax (317) 572-4002.

Wiley also publishes its books in a variety of electronic formats. Some content that appears in print may not be available in electronic formats. For more information about Wiley products, visit our web site at www.wiley.com.

Library of Congress Cataloging-in-Publication Data is Available:

ISBN: 9781394178490 (cloth)
ISBN: 9781394178506 (ePub)
ISBN: 9781394178513 (ePDF)

Cover Design: Wiley
Cover Image: © ihsanyildizli/Getty Images
SKY10048971_060923

This book is dedicated to all my teachers in all the forms they have taken in my life, who helped me discover that questioning, knowing, and seeing are endeavors of the highest order, made truly useful only by the addition of soul and compassion.

Contents

Foreword   ix
Preface   xiii

SECTION I   Abundance Leadership

1   My Journey to Abundance Leadership   3

2   How Abundance Leaders Think   19
Looking for Explanations   19
Optimism   25
Three Other Fields That Inform Abundance Leadership   30

3   Four Meta-Competencies   43
Visioning for the Greater Good   48
Visibility   56
Self-Awareness   58
Managing Well   60

SECTION II   Organizational Health and Abundance Leadership

4   Improving Your Organization's Health   65

5   Macrolevers   69
Charrettes   69
Four-Day Workweek   73
Workspace Design   75
Managing by Circadian Rhythm   77

6 Microlevers: Small Tools for Big Change   87

   The Gong   88

   The Annual Donation: Collective Competition for the Greater Good 89

   Public Agenda: Speak Up and Get Heard   90

   Community Wall: Life Outside of Work   90

   Snow Globes and Collective Memory   91

   Facilitation Rotation   92

   Dream List: Imagining Our Ideal World   92

SECTION III   The How-to Manual

7 Visioning   99

   Visioning   100

   Creativity   107

8 Visibility   113

9 Self-Awareness   117

   Reflection and Affect   121

   Interpersonal Adeptness   135

   Morality   140

   Ego Control   141

10 Managing Well   145

   Team Building   146

   Communication   153

   Protection   157

   Decision-Making   163

Epilogue   169

Appendix A: Additional Resources   171

Appendix B: Organizational Development Bibliography   173

References   181

Acknowledgments   187

About the Author   189

Index   191

Foreword

When Laura Freebairn-Smith walked into my class 40 years ago she was a fiery, red-headed, passionate activist enrolled to learn about management. She has gained some gray hair and a great deal of experience and wisdom while remaining a passionate activist. This book presents what her life has taught her about leadership and effective organization. It has been quite a life. Laura grew up within a family committed to political and spiritual change. Before she came to the management school she had spent years (not days or weeks) working in a refugee camp on the Thai-Cambodia border. She has led an organization development department in a large university and now leads her own consulting firm with the daily reality of bottom-line responsibility. As a result, the book is filled with a wealth of ideas, suggestions, and examples for anyone in a leadership role who aspires to inspire.

But there is more. Laura's book is about a fundamental value proposition: her belief, supported by her own research as well as that of others, that the key to a healthy organization and to effective management is a mindset. She contrasts a view of the world (and the people in it) that focuses on *scarcity* with one that focuses on *abundance* and makes a compelling case that viewing organizational life through the lens of *abundance* yields significantly greater personal and professional health and well-being. In Laura's view, organizational health is itself a complex and nuanced concept that includes everything from employee satisfaction and joy to financial stability and growth.

Part of the power of this book is the idea of a mental model. Not long ago, many of us would have scoffed at the idea that organizational effectiveness rests on the mental model that its members, and especially those in leadership positions, carry around in their heads, preferring to put our faith in financial and statistical models. But this book extends a 40-year exploration of precisely this idea, tying together work on optimism and pessimism in the field of organizational development and economics to make the argument that indeed our mental models have a profound influence on our capacity to lead and inspire.

The other source of the book's impact is the energy and professional life of the author herself. Since that day years ago when Laura walked into my class we have stayed in touch. During the last decade or more I have repeatedly referred individuals and organizations to Laura's firm, Organizational Performance Group, because, quite frankly, she is one of the few practitioners whose integrity and honesty I trust. Throughout the book Laura offers examples from her practice and from the ways in which she leads her own organization. You can take these examples to the bank. They are valuable and trustworthy, fully deserving of the reflection that the book invites each of us to do. And, in addition to the concrete examples from her work, Laura provides us with a glimpse of her own mind, rich with insight and possibility but also filled with the same struggles, personal and professional, that we all recognize.

A book that lays out a new mental model for approaching organizational functioning and leadership action will challenge every reader in some way. A therapist of mine once offered me a simple and different way of viewing the world, one that he was confident would bring me a greater measure of peace. I was aghast at his suggestion that I merely choose to see the world differently because such a choice seemed to me to be supremely difficult (given, of course, that I had already chosen and held tightly to the worldview I already had). In the face of my protest about how hard and perhaps impossible his suggestion was to implement he replied, "I said it was a simple choice, not an easy one." The same could be said of Laura's Abundance Leadership model. Her suggestion to us is that if we can be successful at making this choice to think about the work differently than most of us do now, our capacity to lead others toward a collective goal will be enhanced. And she presents evidence to support her suggestion.

Anyone with responsibility for the work lives of others will learn something important and valuable in this book. The section on abundance behavior in leadership roles, the section on team development, and the section on microlevers for change are chock-full of concrete examples. The book is notable for what a colleague once called *actionable knowledge*, insights and ideas that translate into everyday practice (check out the section on the daily, weekly, and monthly rhythms of a work group, for example).

This book is not the equivalent of being with Laura for a day or working with her organization for a morning. No book could substitute for the experience of interacting with her mind and with the organization that she and her colleagues have created. But it is quite a good approximation, worth the time and energy required to take the deep dive Laura hopes we will take and then to adapt our reflective understanding to the challenges each of us faces in our leadership roles.

David Berg
Yale School of Medicine

Preface

What we think, we become.

—BUDDHA

We are what we pretend to be, so we must be careful about what we pretend to be.

—KURT VONNEGUT JR.

Power doesn't corrupt, it reveals.

—ROY HEATH

There are so many models for leadership, so much written. It matters so much to us as human beings who our leaders are. Our well-being, our safety, our ability to reproduce—all primal needs—are in the hands of leaders. Leaders of our countries, companies, religious organizations, schools. How hard this is these days to feel safe in the hands of our leaders. There are so few beacons of light in leadership roles.

Leaders are also feeling the crush of expectations, as is everyone, to be perfect. These expectations have hit an absurd level. People judge others and their leaders in ways they would never want to be judged.

Even so, can't we expect better and more from our leaders? Can't we have leaders who are able to control their egos, manage what power does to them, and find creative ways to transform our organizations, which have been functioning under the same paradigm (a hierarchical capitalist one) for the last few millennia? Can't we do better?

Maybe. I'm not sure.

I've led small organizations or departments for most of my professional life (over 40 years now), starting at 21 in the Khao-I-Dang refugee camp on the Thai-Cambodian border, where I spent four years working in the International Rescue Committee's Education Program. I left there after serving as the education coordinator for the camp, and another camp called Sakaeo, with a staff of 10 to 20 expatriates and up to 1,000 Cambodian staff members.

My management and leadership journey found me at Yale next, in its master's in public and private management program (later changed to an MBA). The program changed many of my basic understandings of how the world works, layering these ideas on top of an idealism bred by a family of radical social justice activists. I always imagined my father must have thought I was going to the dark side to get an MBA, but it was at least better than becoming a lawyer in his eyes.

After leaving Yale, I became a managing director, chief operating officer, and the head of organizational development for Yale, leading different size staffs at each moment. As I write this book, I'm a managing partner at a small consulting firm, Organizational Performance Group, with a staff of ten who work with leaders of organizations, ranging from Brazilian presidential candidates to three-person nonprofits, trying to improve reading in the inner city.

Throughout my career, I have been a leader who creates strong, often polar, reactions in staff members. *Nice* is not a term that is used to describe me. Not *mean*, but exceptionally direct and quick-witted, expecting those around me to keep up. Having served as a COO and managing director, and focusing on accounting and finance at Yale, then getting a PhD in organizational systems, my mind works quickly. *Demanding* is a term often applied to me, as well as *inspiring* for those who find working with me meaningful. As one of my former staff members said over lunch a few years ago, "Every day, I ask myself, 'What would Laura do?'"

I share this personal journey because I don't think it's easy to be a leader. I have former staff members who hate me, ones who love me, and very few in between. I say things that many leaders might not; I'm open about my opinions and beliefs, and I don't suffer ill-informed comments easily. I studied philosophy at UC Berkeley for my undergraduate degree and excelled in the course on logic, so I want solid arguments, not mush. However, I would say that I have opinions but I avoid judging unless it is called for in a situation.

Most leadership models paint an idealized, walk-on-water type of person as the ideal leader, which leaves us feeling inadequate. The Abundance Leadership model, offered in this book, paints this picture as well because the research shows which leadership behaviors produce better outcomes for organizations. Models are often ideals, not reality. In our immersion program, the instructional staff spend a great deal of time working with participants on how to accept and work with their "perfect imperfections," as John Legend says. We also work on how to surround yourself with people who complement your skills and with whom you resonate. I have never seen a reason why a leader should keep someone around if they don't get along. Really, why? Why spend all that energy navigating a difficult interpersonal fit?

Of course, stating the obvious: we want people around who disagree with us, who question our logic, our math, our impact, but that doesn't mean we can't get along with those people. And we certainly don't want people disagreeing with us all the time.

One of the takeaways of this book is don't feel bad about populating your top team with people with whom you have a synergy. Just be careful that they represent diverse functional and worldviews.

So leading is a bear. My experience from leading my own teams, and teaching and consulting with thousands of leaders, is that only about 10% of people take to leading and managing naturally, a combination of their innate character, life experiences, and training. This is not based on a rigorous study (which would be an interesting one), just my experience. I'd say there's another 25% of leaders and managers who learn to enjoy it and get better at it. They study hard, seek out feedback, work on changing their behavior, go back for more feedback, and keep growing. They don't take it lightly, and they bring their heart and soul to it, leading with compassionate and visionary direction.

All of these leaders, the 35% who get traction—not in terms of money or power but in terms of positive impact on their staff members, their organizations, and their world—work hard to bring their morality, self-awareness, transparency, and deep generosity to the leadership table. Dedicated managers and leaders continually work to create exceptional ecosystems of energy. This is not an easy undertaking, and there are no simple or perfectly right answers. Compassion and generosity help. The Abundance Leadership model encourages this deep courageous leadership.

This book describes the Abundance Leadership model and how it can help you become a better leader, with impact beyond your own organization. The flow of this book is from my background that created the model, to the model itself and the four meta-competencies, then to ways to make your organization healthier and more abundant. I then provide a how-to manual with detailed tips and techniques for the behaviors of an Abundance leader.

The tools for making your organization healthier are divided into two types: microlevers and macrolevers. Microlevers are small, relatively easy to implement tactics you can use to signal the culture you want to create in your organization. Macrolevers are larger policy and practice changes that require more lift to implement but can profoundly alter your employees' experience and productivity.

If the Abundance Leadership model doesn't resonate for you, I encourage you to find a model that does or blend many models. Models offer us ways to make sense of our world and ways to improve it.

We can make the world better. Let's change old leadership paradigms. Let's spread the wealth. Let's spread knowledge. We are in this together. Chief Seattle, chief of the Duwamish and Suquamish tribes, said in a speech, "This we know. The earth does not belong to man; man belongs to the earth. This we know. All things are connected like the blood which unites one family. All things are connected" (Seattle 2023).

I hope you find encouragement for your journey in this book.

SECTION

I

Abundance Leadership

Research is formalized curiosity. It is poking and prying
with a purpose.

—Zora Neale Hurston

In this section, I share how I came to develop the Abundance Leadership
model, based on both in-depth research and my own experience working for others and being a leader. I share this journey for several reasons.
Self-awareness and self-reflection are essential habits of Abundance
leaders. More important, I hope that you will find time to look back on
your professional journey to discover what types of work, what types of
bosses, what types of colleagues, and what types of organizations are
creating meaning for you in your life. Which of those give you energy
and make you feel you are spending your "one precious life" in a way that
matters to you?

Exploring your own journey will help you bring your authentic professional (not authentic personal) self to your role as a leader.

CHAPTER 1

My Journey to Abundance Leadership

Your work is to discover your work and then with all your heart to give yourself to it.

—Buddha

One day I was in a conversation with a colleague about our families and work. As I described most of my immediate family's jobs and professions, I realized that all of us worked for ourselves. I hadn't thought much about that conversation until I started writing this book and thinking about leadership and how hard leading is. Because of these discussions with my family and the reasons for their self-employment, I became aware of how hard it is to lead in a way that makes work fulfilling for others, and why the Abundance Leadership model emerged from my work experience and my educational journey.

To help myself better understand how I came to think about why an Abundance mental model could be a driving force in good leaders, I reflected on my own work journey to my role today, as a partner at Organizational Performance Group (OPG). Similar to many of you readers, I started work early, at the age of 12, with babysitting and small tasks for neighbors and friends of my parents.

In my mid-teens I had two jobs that have always stayed with me. The first was flipping burgers in a small burger shack at the beach where I grew up, Muir Beach (see Figure 1.1). The burger shack was in a converted trailer. There was often only one of us working at a time. Whoever was there would not only make the burgers but also take the cash, make the milkshakes, clean the counters, and more. I had to serve in all roles at different moments.

FIGURE 1.1   Laura at the window of the burger shack at Muir Beach in 1974, age 15.

SOURCE: Laura Freebairn-Smith (Author).

I remember the burger shack boss being very trusting and gone quite often. I cannot visualize him any longer, but I remember the general effect of being left on my own, which felt both good and a little worrisome.

This ability to develop staff members, sometimes by pushing them to the edge of discomfort, shows up in the Abundance Leadership model.

The second job that I had as a teenager was working in a factory that produced goods for head shops, for about $1.65/hour. For those of you who are too young to know what a head shop is, it was a store that sold things like roach clips, bongs, rolling papers, posters, and other 1960s and 1970s weed and hippie paraphernalia. This factory produced the roach clips, the bongs, and other items sold in such shops. The factory took up about half a floor of a big building in the industrial area of Sausalito, one of the towns in Northern California where I grew up. The boss was an older man who was neither curmudgeonly nor nice as I recall; he was matter of fact and focused on productivity. I started out filling orders for stores, walking among the shelves full of bins of paraphernalia.

FIGURE 1.2   Henry Winkler as Fonzi.

SOURCE: AA Film Archive/Allstar Picture Library Ltd/Alamy Stock Photo.

One day the factory got an order to roll thousands of Fonzi posters (see Figure 1.2). If you've ever bought a poster, it probably came rolled up in a long, thin plastic bag. There is a special machine for rolling posters and putting them in those plastic bags (see Figure 1.3). You sit on a stool and use a foot lever to cause a long metal bar to spin. The bar is right above your lap. The stack of unrolled posters is on the other side of the bar. You take a poster and begin wrapping it around the bar and then, guiding the poster with your hand, you step on the foot lever that activates the rod to roll. Once the poster is rolled, you take a plastic bag and pull it over the end of the rod and the poster. Slide the poster off the rod into the bag. Tuck the end of the plastic bag into the top of the poster and put the completed poster into a box.

I was so fast at rolling Fonzi posters, which were being sold at the local Safeway store, that the boss promoted me into the glass-blowing shop where bongs were made. I learned how to make glass bongs in the last few months of that job. I can't remember why I stopped working

FIGURE 1.3   Pedal-operated poster rolling machine.

SOURCE: Boggs Equipment.

there; maybe it was a summer job. What has stuck with me through the years were the promotions for being productive. I remember so clearly the pride I took in being the fastest and being promoted. Celebration, reward, and recognition are also key techniques for Abundance leaders.

I had many other odd jobs during my early years. Similar to many students, I waitressed for a summer and fall semester at a restaurant near Fisherman's Wharf in San Francisco. I would work on the weekends while I was attending UC Berkeley. On occasion I would work the overnight shift, which was one of my favorites. I loved the early morning customers, some of them fishermen heading out onto the Bay to fish. I also loved bringing home apple pie to my father's apartment in San Francisco where I was staying and eating it with him right before I would go to bed, and he would head off to work.

The restaurant was a non-unionized environment. At some point the union was conducting an organizing effort and the staff members were asked to go out on strike, which we did. It was my first time becoming a union member and the only time I would walk a picket line. I would become a union member again much later when I was a professor at

Central Connecticut State University. This early experience with walking a picket line and unionization was an integral part of my education and evolution as a leader.

Unions and picket lines would reappear in my first weeks at Yale, when the clerical and technical staff members went out on strike just as the fall semester started in my first year of graduate school. I have complex opinions about unions that are not the topic of this book. Suffice it to say, I think they are essential in some industries, and I think they need to transform the way they work with management in other industries.

Abundance leaders are thinking about bigger societal and environmental issues such as income equality, empowering workers, and other matters that will improve the world, not just their own lives.

The next significant work memory I have is a very short stint I did as a business manager for a construction firm in Oakland right after I graduated from Berkeley, while I was waiting to head to Asia that fall. This was another piece in the leadership mosaic of my work life that produced the Abundance Leadership model.

At the construction company, the entire workforce was male; it was 1980 after all. I don't begrudge the context of history; it is what it was. One of the remarkable things about this job was the thinly veiled sexualized photographs on the walls of the office. The owner was an amateur photographer who took pictures with soft filters of scantily clothed women. Similar to many women of my age, we learned how to navigate a sexually fraught environment. That is not the topic of this book, but I will say that sexual overtures, physical touching, and more were common in my work experience until the late 1990s.

Abundance leaders work hard to ensure that their staff members feel safe and work in non-abusive conditions, the definitions of which are in constant flux and evolution.

I left the job in Oakland to go trekking in the Solo-Khumbu region of Nepal to the base camp of Everest with my mother. The trip was a graduation gift from her. Although not a work-related experience, two events during that trek would inform my thinking about leadership in the coming years.

There were 25 of us on that trek—a large group. In Nepal in the high Himalayas, there are no roads once you get above a certain altitude, and the trails are narrow. By the end of each day, the person at the front of the line could be two to three hours ahead of the person at the back of the line. Our trek leader was a young woman named Meredith. She had a habit of moving up and down the line all day long. She always made sure that she or a Sherpa was with the last person in line. She had a marvelous quiet, steady presence that was very reassuring—always making sure the last person had support. We use this method of leading, attending to all, in the Abundance Leadership immersion program during one of the experiential exercises. This method of leading is important in day-to-day work as well.

The second event on that trek that changed my internal relationship to service and leading was when I contracted pneumonia at 10,000 feet. Most days I was one of the first into camp because of my age—I was the youngest at 21. One day I found that it was getting harder and harder to breathe. I would walk 100 steps and have to sit down. I arrived into camp two to three hours after the last person, accompanied by my mother and a Sherpa. That night I had a high fever; the doctor on the trek came to our tent and gave me a shot of antibiotics. The next morning, I was still very sick.

That day, the Sherpas created a way to carry me on their backs, using a tumpline and a stick (see Figure 1.4). A Sherpa would carry me for 20 minutes, and then pass me to another Sherpa. Up in the Himalayas,

FIGURE 1.4   A woman carries firewood using a tumpline.

SOURCE: Sergey Pashko / Wikimedia Commons / CC BY 3.0.

there is very little flat ground. We were going up and down all day. The Sherpas were always polite and kind and never made me feel like a burden, which I clearly was both literally and figuratively. The Sherpas were moving so fast that the doctor fell and broke his wrist while trying to keep up with us. I remember crying on the backs of the Sherpas out of humility and gratitude. It was a wonderful teaching about what service means, a teaching that would serve me well in my work in the refugee camps. A core competency of Abundance leaders is the ability to express kindness and compassion easily.

I left Nepal and flew to Bangkok. Serving as the education coordinator for the International Rescue Committee (IRC) in the refugee camps, Khao-I-Dang (Figure 1.5) and Sakaeo, was my next job, and one of my most profound work experiences. My first boss in Khao-I-Dang, Dan Steinbock, gave me significant responsibility for a 21-year-old. He saw potential in my energy and focus. As a result, I moved from an education assistant position to education coordinator (the American equivalent of

FIGURE 1.5   Cambodian refugee at work in Khao-I-Dang refugee camp in the early 1980s.

SOURCE: Laura Freebairn-Smith (Author).

FIGURE 1.6   Office entry sign in Khao-I-Dang refugee camp.

SOURCE: Laura Freebairn-Smith (Author).

school superintendent) in about a year and a half (Figures 1.6 and 1.7). By the time I left Thailand. I was supervising 10 or so Thai and expatriate staff members and more than 1,000 Cambodian staff members. In Khao-I-Dang, the education program served more than 20,000 refugees, with 13 primary schools, kindergartens, an arts center, the only Cambodian printing press in the world at that time, a woodworking training program, and more (see Figure 1.8).

As education coordinator, I reported to an IRC boss in Bangkok, a four-hour drive away. I frequently reported to the United Nations High Commissioner for Refugees (UNHCR) representatives in Bangkok as well, so my bosses were somewhat remote. This pattern of self-management or hands-off supervision would become a pattern in my life. Toward the end of my four years working on the border, I began to experience burnout and frustration. I knew I needed to make a change.

After Thailand and the refugee camps, I left to attend Yale to get my MBA. My summer internship, done between the two years of the MBA program, was at the World Bank creating spreadsheets that would predict the cost of building hospitals in Nigeria. My two supervisors were

FIGURE 1.7   Children in class in Khao-I-Dang refugee camp.

SOURCE: Laura Freebairn-Smith (Author).

gone most of the internship. My memory is not completely accurate, but I think I saw them maybe four to five times that summer, so I was left to my own devices to sit in an office and stare at Excel spreadsheets for the summer. This was another moment in my life when my boss was not particularly present. There are pros and cons to this hands-off/absentee leadership, but I missed being part of a team.

Abundance leaders look to build teams, ensuring that everyone feels included.

After Yale I got a job as a chief operating officer for a very small non-profit. I was not a good personality fit with the two leaders, who had a particularly symbiotic relationship. There is literature about triads as a problematic configuration, with triangulation occurring. I think that was part of the problem, as was just a general difference of personalities and my own professional immaturity. I was just beginning to gain a much more sophisticated view of organizational life.

Being aware of team dynamics, and one's relationships' impact on those around you, is a highly advanced skill in Abundance Leadership.

FIGURE 1.8   Laura with her Cambodian staff in Khao-I-Dang refugee camp.

SOURCE: Laura Freebairn-Smith (Author).

I then became the managing director of the Gesell Institute in New Haven (see Figures 1.9 and 1.10). The day that I started the job, at the age of 28, I found the following items on my desk or in my inbox: a note from the bookkeeper saying there was not enough cash for payroll, the resignation letter of the executive director, a bank statement showing that much of the endowment funds had been depleted, and three or four other critical items that put the organization in jeopardy. When I teach leadership, sometimes I use that inbox as a case study.

Over the next two years, I would spend my time helping the Institute go from 67 staff members down to 5, working myself out of a job as well. Ultimately, 30 years later, the Institute has become part of Yale and is now on solid ground again, thanks to new leadership.

That work at the Institute was what I would call my third master's degree: my first being the work in the refugee camps, and my second being my MBA from Yale. At the Institute, I worked with the executive

FIGURE 1.9   Institute's offices at 310 Prospect Street, New Haven, CT.

SOURCE: Tzurin/Wikimedia Commons.

FIGURE 1.10   Dr. Arnold Gesell.

SOURCE: Herbert Gehr/The LIFE Picture Collection/Shutterstock.com.

director who had resigned for the first two weeks of my job. I then worked with a board member who stepped in as executive director but was asked to step down shortly afterwards due to a variety of issues with his leadership. Last, I reported directly to the board as the Institute got smaller and smaller.

The complexities of closing down a 40-year-old institution that was failing long before I showed up provided lessons in ownership, leadership, group dynamics, theft, anger, and being misrepresented in the press. I remember a quote in the local paper being attributed to me but the quote was something that a former leader had said. That was an early lesson in misrepresentation in the public sphere. In a crisis,

Abundance leaders work hard to stay calm and unruffled. I can't say I succeeded at this at such a young age but this situation gave me a great deal of early practice.

The Gesell Institute job was another work situation in which I had intermittent bosses, no bosses, and semi-effective bosses. As this pattern of working without a consistent or nearby boss continued, I began to realize that it suited me to be my own boss, and the pattern was stimulating my thinking about leadership.

After my work at Gesell, I started my first consulting firm, Good Work Associates (GWA), which I ran for 10 years. In the ninth year, I told my business partner that I needed to step down and see what I wanted to do next. One of my last consulting jobs at GWA was to do a whitepaper for Peter Vallone, the head of human resources at Yale at that time.

Peter asked me to do some research and benchmarking on what a good organizational development (OD) department or function at Yale might be. I did the research for him and presented a paper that looked at what Harvard and other Ivy League institutions were doing in the OD arena, as well as places like Disney. I presented my findings and suggested that Yale start an organizational development unit. They created the unit and a position for an organizational development lead.

Peter asked me if I wanted the job. I initially declined because I was not yet sure if I wanted to continue in the field of OD or where I wanted to work. After some negotiating, I said yes to the job. Peter turned out to be one of the best bosses I have had in my career. I had a boss whom I got along with, and respected, and who deeply respected my expertise. I had had some of those attributes in prior bosses but not all of them in one boss. It was working with Peter and other leaders at Yale that were the nutrients that brought the seeds of Abundance Leadership to life.

I remember asking Peter once if he wanted to attend a meeting with the provost with me. He said, "Why would I do that? You're the expert." He had another phrase that enabled him to delegate while also calling his staff members to pay attention to what they were doing and when and how to keep him informed, but not micro-managing us. He would say, "I don't want to read something in the headlines that I don't know about." This was such a good guideline for making decisions and for keeping him informed. Peter retired in my fourth year in that position.

Abundance Leaders grow staff in many ways, including delegation.

There were many other people and experiences at Yale that informed my view of leadership and gave me inspiration for what women can do as leaders. Two women stand out to me: Linda Lorimer and Alison Richard. Linda was the secretary for the university. This role is not that of administrative assistant but serves as a critical strategic advisor to the president. This role oversees the board of trustees among other major committees and functions. Richard Levin, president of Yale at that time, trusted Linda deeply. She was energetic, dedicated to Yale, and visionary. And, she was action-oriented and decisive.

I went to see her about some funding to revise new employee orientation. I came prepared with all kinds of documents, analysis, and other items to support the need for extra funding. She asked me one or two questions, asked how much I needed, and said fine. The entire meeting took 15 minutes. It was delightful!

The other leader who left a lasting impression on me was Alison Richard, then provost of Yale. She would go on to become the first female vice chancellor of Cambridge University. She was always calm, available, and thorough. Standing barely 5 feet tall, she never lacked gravitas or presence. Her quiet and calm demeanor grounded the entire room. She and I worked on a few initiatives together, and in hindsight I imagine I seemed overly energetic and somewhat unformed as a professional to her, even though I was in my late 30s. But she never made me feel that way. I felt that she trusted me, my competence, and my expertise. She was lovely to work with, and when she left for Cambridge, I felt that a critical piece of my pantheon of stars that supported my work at Yale was gone.

Both Linda and Alison modeled Abundance Leadership behaviors of decisiveness and being calm and unruffled.

I had other experiences as the leader of the Learning Center at Yale that continue to inform my view of what worked and didn't work as a leader. One of those experiences was the day the twin towers fell. I was six months pregnant with my second son, sitting in a meeting with the university librarian, when a worker came in and said that one of the twin towers had been hit by a jet. We were dismayed and concerned but we assumed it was a one-off accident, as so many people all over the world did until 40 minutes later when the second plane hit the other tower.

The worker came back in and told us about the second tower. After a short huddle, I set off on foot across campus to get back to my office to gather my 20 or so staff members I had at that time. We gathered in one of the conference rooms and we talked about what had just happened and spent a very brief period processing our fear and our emotions. At the end of that discussion, I told everyone to go home. I did not consult with my boss or with the university policy or with anyone else. I trusted my intuition and my instinct, and I knew that everyone needed to go get their children, find their partners, and be with their families because we had no idea what was happening to the country at that moment.

Abundance leaders display compassion and are decisive, especially in a crisis.

Another experience at Yale that highlighted an Abundance Leadership behavior involved staff members' acute awareness of my affect. While I was at Yale, after Peter Vallone had retired, the new VP of HR told us that we needed to downsize. All of the HR directors, of which I was one, and the VP would meet regularly in a building across the street from my office. I found out later that my staff members would wait at the window, watching as I would return from these meetings to see what my physical and facial affect were. They were trying to see if it was good news or bad news.

As the Abundance Leadership model articulates later in this book, our awareness of our physical and facial affect is a critical part of being a good leader. This moment at Yale was an early lesson in that insight.

Another experience at Yale, that shows up as a behavior in the Abundance Leadership model, is advocating for your staff members in a variety of settings. I remember sitting in a meeting at Yale talking about an open position for which an African American staff member was qualified to move up into. Recently three other positions had been given to white staff members without requiring an interview process. In that particular meeting, it was suggested that the African American staff member should go through an interview process. I objected, pointing out that the three white staff members had been appointed without even a review of a résumé as far as I knew. The conversation came to a dead stop and the decision was made to give the African American staff member the position.

The last experience I had at Yale that I want to share was the catalyst for my conducting research on and creating the Abundance Leadership model. During my last year or so at Yale, I worked with John Pepper, the former CEO of Procter & Gamble. He is a Yale alum and was recently retired. President Levin had asked him to come back to Yale for a few years to help modernize some of the administrative functions.

John was a dedicated organizational development fan, having seen the positive impact of organizational development work at Procter & Gamble. He and I hit it off immediately. Again, I felt deeply respected for my energy, competence, and expertise.

One of the most salient memories I have of John's deep kindness and humility is when we were walking down a hallway at Yale on the way to a meeting. We came across a service and maintenance worker pushing a cart of cleaning supplies. John, although running slightly late for the meeting, stopped to speak to the service and maintenance worker. John introduced himself, asked the worker their name, and asked how their work was going and what they needed to do their job better. It was such a great moment with no artifice. John followed up later and made sure the worker knew that their suggestions had been acted on. The sensation of working with John was that anything was possible. He became one of the sources of inspiration for Abundance Leadership.

I stayed another three years at Yale, after Peter left, with bosses who were not great fits for me as I came to realize that my relentlessly challenging and entrepreneurial stance can feel antagonistic to people who supervise me. After seven years in my role as director of the Organizational Development and Learning Center, and declining a higher-level role at Yale, I once again resumed consulting, five years later merging my consulting firm with Tony Panos's firm, to create OPG. Along the way, I completed my doctorate, producing the Abundance Leadership model through my research.

Each work experience, combined with exceptional teachers and educational opportunities, led me to conceive of the Abundance Leadership model. These experiences also helped me be a better resource for my clients, my staff members, my community, and my family.

I encourage you to take a moment to reflect on your own journey, and see where Abundance behaviors and values have already appeared, and where you might bring them more fully into your life and work.

CHAPTER 2

How Abundance Leaders Think

Management is doing things right; leadership is doing the right thing.

—PETER F. DRUCKER

As I had to come realize on my own journey, and as my doctoral research confirmed, some leaders create more energy, joy, productivity, and dedication in their staff members than others. About these bosses, people would say, "I loved working for them." For many of us, when asked to remember a boss for whom we loved to work, we can immediately conjure up someone; the memory of working for them brings a smile to our face. Sometimes we can be articulate about one or two particular behaviors the boss exhibited that made them so great to work for; sometimes it's an overall attitude or approach of the boss.

An Abundance Leadership Immersion Program alumni captured the essence of an Abundance leader: "I think of Abundance Leadership very similarly to how I feel about Leadership from the Inside Out by Kevin Cashman. While the tools and the context in which it is provided are as a business tool or a management tool, it is in fact, a personal tool, or a guidebook, as to how you can live, authentically in your personal life and let that flow into your work life. Better people make better leaders. I think saying this explicitly can help people along the journey."

LOOKING FOR EXPLANATIONS

When I began my doctoral work, I could not find a leadership model that adequately encompassed the range of leadership behaviors that sum up the felt experience by staff members of great bosses, nor did existing models examine the mental models that drive those behaviors. Leadership research has tried to explain this phenomenon with numerous conceptual models. Is it the personality of the leader? Social stature? Training? Context? The research has evolved over time to explain great leaders as a mix of personality, experience, context, and serendipity, but I could not find one that explained what was creating these positive experiences. So I did my doctoral research to figure it out, and I found that mental models are a critical driver of beliefs and behaviors.

"Mental models are deeply ingrained assumptions, generalizations, or even pictures of images that influence how we understand the world and how we take action."

—*Peter Senge (1990)*

Our mental models affect what we notice, how we react to what we experience, and how we interpret information. Mental models are the intellectual road maps we use to navigate our observed and felt environments, and, as maps, they highlight some elements of the environment and information while excluding others (Mathieu et al. 2000).

For example, when I ask undergraduate students to draw a map of the route they take between their home and college, the map is most detailed at the ends of the journey and usually only has one or two key signposts along the way. Each student's map of the college emphasizes a different element. For one student it is the parking lot, for another it is the student center.

Essentially, mental models are organized knowledge structures that enable individuals to interact with their environment. Specifically, mental models enable people to predict and explain the behavior of the world around them, to recognize and remember relationships among components of the environment, and to construct expectations for what is likely to occur next (Rouse and Morris 1986). Furthermore, mental models enable people to draw inferences, make predictions, understand phenomena, decide which actions to take, and experience events vicariously (Johnson-Laird 1983). Mental models serve three crucial purposes: they help people to describe, explain, and predict events in their environment (Mathieu and Godwin 2000: 274).

Deeper mental models—the models that explain the world and dictate how we interact with it—arise out of both genetics and personality. We are each born with a distinct personality that is further molded by our environment. This blend of our innate and developed selves gives rise to our deepest mental models and beliefs about many critical aspects of our lives (McCrae and Ostendorf 2000). Is the world a safe place or a dangerous place? Are people basically good at heart? Is rain a cause for celebration or whining?

In my research, I examined two particular mental models—abundance and scarcity—that I believed dictated a range of leadership behaviors, and which my research confirmed. Abundance and scarcity mental models affect behavior at all levels of a system: from the individual to the leader to the entire ecosystem. On the one hand, when a system is viewed as abundant, fear of scarcity decreases. Sharing increases. However, if the system is seen as limitlessly abundant, waste and disregard occur. On the other hand, scarcity mental models produce hoarding and intra-system stress. If a system is viewed as excessively scarce, violence and intolerance occur.

Individuals have an orientation somewhere on the spectrum between abundance and scarcity; they view their lives, organizations, budgets, or the world as inherently resource rich or inherently resource poor or somewhere on this spectrum. Just as individuals have an abundance or scarcity orientation, so do most sciences and cultures. They have an underlying assumption about the extent of the resources in the system in which they are engaged. The orientation runs along a spectrum from one of scarcity (i.e., there are not enough resources to meet demand) to one of abundance (i.e., there are more than enough resources to meet demand), or myriad steps along the spectrum such as one of adequacy (i.e., there are just enough resources to meet demand).

The scarcity-abundance spectrum is at play in other systems as well, ranging from large, infinite systems to smaller, more bounded systems. For example, the universe and the mind are often viewed as infinite, abundant resources. The planet and its micro-ecosystems are often viewed as finite and prone to scarcity, but they do not have to be viewed as such. Even smaller systems such as individual organizations can be framed as resource-abundant or resource-scarce systems, depending on many factors.

A mental model of scarcity assumes that the resource in question is part of a closed system with limited and insufficient nonrenewable resources. For example, global energy, if viewed only from the perspective of oil reserves, could ultimately create a scarcity mental model because reserves will run out if there are no alternative fuels. If viewed through the lens of wind and solar power, an abundance mental model is possible.

Another manifestation of the scarcity mentality is an assumption that even with abundant resources there are not enough for any particular individual. This is one of the basic human fears—not having enough resources to survive or reproduce. The definition of *enough* is problematic for sustainable systems, as I explore later in this book when I discuss the fields of economics and sustainability. *Enough* has different meanings to different people based on their experiences and situations. In the Cambodian refugee camp where I worked, on a daily basis the refugees consumed probably one-half of the food and water that the Western staff members did. To the Cambodians, after years of starvation under Pol Pot, the water and food was abundant. To the Western relief workers, it seemed insufficient.

I believe that the labeling of any system as either resource-scarce or resource-abundant depends greatly on the individual perceiver's bias, assumptions, power, and knowledge. To build on a previous example, if a person focuses only on oil as an energy source, then the planet is an energy resource–scarce system. If a person focuses on renewable energy sources, the planet appears as energy-abundant, as an almost energy-infinite system. Where we focus affects our view.

"Focusing only on oil means all the eggs are in one basket. Focusing on renewable energy means diversification. I think this diversification is key in the shift toward an abundant mental model"

—*K. Laszlo, (personal communication, October 10, 2005)*

Abundance and scarcity orientations have serious implications for science, cultures, organizations, people, and the planet because they affect behavior. My review of the literature showed that the scarcity-abundance spectrum has affected such disparate fields as economics, sustainability, philosophy, organizational behavior, and politics (Adams 2000; Covey 1999; Malthus 1797/1993; Perry and Griggs 1997; Rossatto 2005). These mental models affect leadership and organizational culture and outcomes.

At the time of my doctoral research, there was little research available on leadership abundance mental models. My research set out to rectify that. My research showed that scarcity and abundance models in leaders affect their behaviors concerning financial resources, promotion, power, recognition, control, kindness, respect, and more. As I began my research, I expected to see Abundance leaders exhibit more of the following behaviors:

- Inspiring
- Sharing information
- Listening
- Protecting staff members from abusive conditions
- Asking for resources for staff members
- Delegating
- Sharing the limelight
- Keeping criticism to a minimum
- Giving high levels of praise
- Having faith in good outcomes
- Expressing compassion and kindness
- Thinking in the long term
- Encouraging creativity
- Acting locally but thinking globally
- Thinking about whole systems
- Learning
- Focusing on being, not only on doing and having
    (Adams 2004 for last six items in list)

Scarcity-mentality leadership would exhibit the opposite of these abundance behaviors. However, a leader can be realistic about the limitations of resources and still have an abundance mental model based on optimism about alternative resources and the ability of the staff members or organization to problem-solve. An abundance leader does not pretend there are no problems or limits; the leader conveys the belief that the organization can meet the challenges successfully.

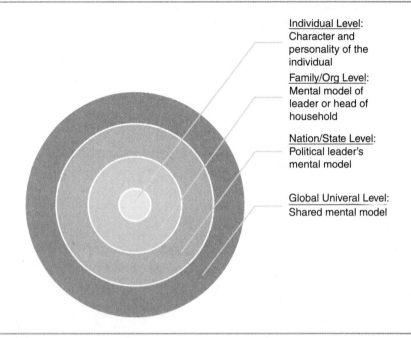

Individual Level:
Character and
personality of the
individual

Family/Org Level:
Mental model of
leader or head of
household

Nation/State Level:
Political leader's
mental model

Global Univeral Level:
Shared mental model

FIGURE 2.1 Embedded layers of mental models.

SOURCE: Laura Freebairn-Smith (Author).

As mentioned, abundance and scarcity orientations are found at all levels of a system: a person has a character-based orientation to abundance; a family has a family-wide orientation; entire organizations have an orientation in one direction or the other. Each element of the system is influenced by the other elements' abundance orientation. Figure 2.1 shows my conceptual map of the confounded and embedded nature of these systems.

Table 2.1 gives more detail about the first level of analysis (individual) in which feelings, beliefs, and behaviors in individuals are found at either end of the abundance-scarcity spectrum. For example, one person might exhibit more courageous behavior on a more consistent basis than another person. Or a person might be prone to stating absolute truths instead of adapting to individual situations. Where optimism and pessimism are surrogates for abundance and scarcity, we see the following:

TABLE 2.1 Proposed Ends of the Scarcity-Abundance Continuum of Emotional Reactions

Extreme	Scarcity	Abundance	Extreme
Paranoia	Fear	Courage	Foolhardiness
Violence	Hate	Compassion	Self-negation
Despair	Hopelessness	Hope	Fantasy or delusion
Irreverence	Disrespect	Respect	Moral relativism; obsequiousness
"Isms" and oppression	Absolutes	Connection to detail, specificity of environment and anomalies	Lack of "big picture" thinking
Negativity	Pessimism	Optimism	Naiveté
Isolation	Solitariness/lack of sense of place in the universe	Faith	Fantasy or Illusion

When people confront adversity or difficulty in their lives, they experience a variety of emotions, ranging from excitement and eagerness, to anger, anxiety, and depression. The balance among these feelings appears to relate to people's degree of optimism or pessimism. (Scheier, Carver, and Bridges 2001: 191)

Table 2.1 shows what might be predicted ranges of individual behaviors. The two middle columns show an expected normal range of reactions to life's events. The outer columns show the extremes of each continuum of reactions. It would seem that individuals would thrive psychologically when they find balance and appropriateness between the two ends of the spectrum. For example, at times a scarcity reaction is appropriate, abundance at other times.

OPTIMISM

One critical aspect of an abundance mental model is optimism. We all have experienced the difference between an encounter with a pessimist and an optimist, one sucks the energy out of a conversation, the other increases the energy. I don't want to confuse critical thinking and judicious analysis with pessimism. The differentiator is the tone of inquiry and the underlying intention of the inquiry.

Positive thinking and optimism are heralded throughout the psychology literature as desirable attributes, ones that produce greater health, better relationships, and better managers. Much has been written about optimism, a character trait that seems to provide numerous benefits for people and is closely correlated to abundance behaviors. Optimism is beautifully defined by Martin Seligman in his description of an optimist.

> *The optimists, who are confronted with the same hard knocks of this world, think about misfortune in the opposite way. They tend to believe defeat is just a temporary setback, that its causes are confined to this one case. The optimists believe defeat is not their fault: Circumstances, bad luck, or other people brought it about. (Seligman 1990: 4–5)*

Optimism is that uncanny ability to see the best and assume the best of the moment and the future. Optimists place the locus of control in the appropriate place, the place that gives them the most hope and the ability to sustain energy and action.

In works such as *The Skills of Encouragement*, we hear the call to be positive:

> *The next time you are with a group of people, look for the encourager. He or she is the one whose arrival lights up the atmosphere, who circulates good news, who mobilizes the resources of each person, and who conveys that energy-giving optimism that raises the group "will" over the "won't." (Dinkmeyer and Losoncy 1996: 1)*

Seligman's work on optimism and pessimism marks a middle point in the research on this topic since the 1940s; it reflects the history of the field but is also referenced in many works that follow. Because optimism is an important element of an abundance mentality, his work also provides a nice backdrop for a partial explanation of the psychological basis of the Abundance Leadership behavior. In Seligman's work I see a launching point for explanations of why some people—and thus some leaders—see the world through a positive abundance mental model versus a negative scarcity mental model (Seligman 1990). His work merits closer examination.

"In the absence of a leader who is optimistic, the staff and the organization can fall into a spiral of despair. Optimism on the part of the leader helps lift the organization and those in it. We have enough examples of things not going well in business and society. The leader needs to move everyone and everything forward."

—*Tony Panos (personal correspondence, January 2023)*

Seligman (1990) argues that there are three important ways people explain events, especially misfortune and good fortune. He calls these our *habits of explanation*. Depending where on the spectrum of each habit you land, this indicates your level of optimism or pessimism. The methods of explanation are permanence, pervasiveness, and personalization.

Permanence has to do with how persistent a person views a problem to be. "People who give up easily believe the causes of the bad events that happen to them are permanent: The bad events will persist, will always be there to affect their lives" (Seligman 1990: 44). Optimistic people see negative circumstances as temporary and thus surmountable; they do not surrender to hopelessness (a core aspect of pessimism). Optimistic people see positive events as more likely to persist. Abundance leaders see bad events as data in a moment in time. The data become the source for change.

The second habit is pervasiveness. "Pervasiveness is about space . . . [Pessimists] catastrophize. When one thread of their lives snaps, the whole fabric unravels" (Seligman 1990: 46). A person can see a problem as pervasive and widespread or discrete and contained. Seligman gives the example in a contrast of two sentences (47):

"All teachers are unfair."
"Professor Seligman is unfair."

The first sentence creates a feeling that all teachers now, in the past, and into the future will be unfair. This in turn creates a sense of fatalism and hopelessness—a classic sign of a pessimist (Seligman 1990). The latter sentence is an optimist's view of the situation. It is only this professor at this moment who is unfair.

The third and final habit that indicates optimism or pessimism is personalization.

> *When bad things happen, we can blame ourselves (internalize) or we can blame other people or circumstances (externalize). People who blame themselves when they fail have low self-esteem as a consequence. . . . People who blame external events do not lose self-esteem when bad events strike. (Seligman 1990: 49)*

Seligman (1990) again gives some examples:

> *"I have no talent at poker." (internal)*
> *"I have no luck at poker." (external)*

Seligman says that personalization controls what we feel, while permanence and pervasiveness control what we do. It is easy to give personalization too much credit for influencing our optimism or pessimism orientation. "Personalization is the only dimension simple to fake. If I tell you to talk about your troubles in an external way now, you will be able to do it" (Seligman 1990: 50). It is harder to switch from seeing things as all pervasive and permanent to seeing them as bounded and time-limited than to depersonalize sources of events (Seligman 1990).

Pessimism is the view that what can go wrong will go wrong consistently over an extended period of time. Pessimists do not imagine an oasis as they trek across a desert. They are certain that every lump is cancer, all people are of ill-will, and no good shall come of it, no matter what the "it" is. To some extent, pessimism correlates to a scarcity mentality but, similar to abundance and optimism, it is not a one-for-one match. A persistently pessimistic leader takes the vibrancy, innovation, and energy out of an organization.

Pessimism, in moderation, serves a crucial role for human beings. Seligman describes pessimism's constructive role in our lives. "Pessimism serves the purpose of pulling us back a bit from the risky exaggerations of our optimism, making us think twice, keeping us from making rash, foolhardy gestures" (Seligman 1990: 114). He makes the important argument that pessimism is fully merited at times, such as when there is great danger involved. Pessimism makes us more risk averse and better at realistically calculating the costs of a decision.

Other authors have built on Seligman's work, and there is a robust body of material on optimism and pessimism. One author in this area, Susan Vaughan, a psychiatrist, focuses on the individual's internal source of optimism. Her argument is that our ability to control feelings without squashing the feelings gives us the capacity for an optimistic view (Vaughan 2000).

Vaughan says that optimism depends on the ability to construct and sustain the illusion of "an island" (a positive end state coming in the near future); optimism is the result of an internal process of illusion building. For example, a person who is undergoing chemotherapy is able to imagine a point in the future when they will be healthy again.

She makes an intriguing argument that being overly connected to reality leads to depression. Vaughan (2000) feels that if we knew the odds against us or the odds of future difficulties, we would be depressed. As an optimist, I found it disheartening to think that reality can be so depressing. As a Buddhist, the thought of ongoing future challenges, ups and downs, seems to be just the natural state of being human, neither positive nor negative.

Vaughan (2000) adds some other nuances to Seligman's work. She points out that optimists persevere. This part of Vaughan's work reminds me of a Marge Piercy poem, "To Be of Use," whose opening stanza so clearly defines the persistence of an optimist:

> The people I love the best
> jump into work head first
> without dallying in the shallows
> and swim off with sure strokes almost out of sight.
> They seem to become natives of that element,
> The black sleek heads of seals
> Bouncing like half-submerged balls.

> (Piercy 1991: 172)

Vaughan (2000) argues that the beacon of hope an optimist maintains must be internal, not just external, because our lens filters reality. Optimism comes from an internal sense of control over our own inner states. This argument is slightly different than Seligman's (1990), who argues that optimism comes from how we make sense of external events.

The exploration of optimism and pessimism mirrors the abundance and scarcity behaviors in leaders. The difference between optimism and abundance is subtle. Intuitively, we might assume that those who see their personal life, organization, or the planet as inherently abundant probably have an optimistic attitude. But abundance orientation is broader than optimism.

Abundance mentality includes behaviors that indicate a lack of fear of scarce resources. Abundance behaviors such as sharing resources (e.g., making donations), believing that things will improve (e.g., seeing the glass as half-full), and creating community (e.g., reaching out to neighbors) indicate a faith in one's ability to do well without hoarding. In organizational life, abundance behaviors include collaborating, offering to help without being asked, creatively problem-solving, and more. These behaviors are not necessarily those of an optimist. One can be optimistic and not abundant, although I would conjecture that this is infrequent.

THREE OTHER FIELDS THAT INFORM ABUNDANCE LEADERSHIP

Making progress toward a better world and better organizations, is of deep concern to Abundance leaders who grapple with questions such as these:

- What constitutes abundance?
- What constitutes progress and when is enough enough?
- How can I and my organization make things better?

To help understand these questions, I looked at three other areas of study to help me develop the abundance leadership model: organizational development, leadership, and economics. First, let's look at what the field of organizational development can contribute to the abundance leadership model.

Given the copious material in psychology on optimism and pessimism (which are close relatives of abundance and scarcity), and given that psychology is one of the two founding fields of organizational behavior, the other being sociology, one might expect to find some material on abundance and scarcity in organizational behavior or development. This was not the case when I was conducting the research in the early 2000s.

OD uses the terms *abundance* and *scarcity* in strategic planning texts and in relatively few other places. The terms used to analyze the environment are best represented in the work of authors such as Michael Porter (1980). Strategic planning texts suggest scanning the environment to see if it is resource rich or resource scarce. In turn, organizations adjust their strategies to adapt to the environmental resource level or decide to go into new environments. These insights seem tangentially related to the concept of abundance leadership.

Moving away from strategic planning texts, the leadership literature, a robust area in OD, did not provide answers to my original questions. I once asked Richard Hackman, an authority in the field of motivation, organization development, and teams, who taught at Harvard University, if he had ever encountered the terms *abundance* or *scarcity* in any depth in the leadership literature. His answer was a resounding no (R. Hackman, personal communication, September 12, 2005). However, there are a few minor pieces worth a look.

Stephen Covey (2015), the guru of effective habits, wrote a brief two-page piece on "primary greatness," which later became a book. It is one of the only texts that I could find at the time of my original research that ties abundance to leadership. Covey has a pop psychology style that saves itself from platitudes by being grounded in a deeply compassionate human ethic, and this style comes through in this small but pithy piece. Covey argues that "primary greatness," the deepest and most sustainable form of greatness, is based on three personality traits: integrity, maturity, and abundance mentality. The last is of interest to this book's topic.

Covey's (2015) definition of "abundance mentality" provides an excellent description of abundance and scarcity behaviors.

Most people are deeply scripted in the scarcity mentality. They see life as a finite pie: If someone gets a big piece of pie, it means less for everyone else—and most importantly, for them. Our thinking should be that there is plenty out there for everybody. This abundance mentality flows out of a deep sense of personal worth and security. It results in sharing recognition, profits and responsibility. It opens up and creates new options and alternatives. It turns personal joy and fulfillment outward. It recognizes unlimited possibilities for positive interactions, growth and development. (219)

Covey (1999) also suggests that a combination of humility, courage, and integrity produces wisdom and an abundance mentality. Covey goes on to suggest the source of the scarcity mentality so many people have.

I think the reason why so many people buy into the scarcity mind-set is because they grow up with conditional love. Love makes the world go round, and if from early childhood your feelings of worth and acceptance come from comparison and competition, the scarcity mind-set is wired into you. (13)

Here Covey is skating on thin theoretical ice because of his focus on nurture alone. Seligman and others would argue that two children from the same household can have different pessimism and optimism orientations. In psychology, the hypothesized sources of these behaviors are both nature and nurture (Seligman 1990). Covey's argument that abundance mentality comes only from the nurture side of the equation goes against a substantial body of psychology research.

Leadership research and studies were helpful in developing the Abundance Leadership model. Leadership occupies a significant part of the American psyche and thus, since the mid-1900s, a significant part of the management literature, and yet researchers still wonder if leadership matters.

The studies . . . in this article would leave readers in little doubt that leaders do matter—to their organizations and to their followers—they do make a difference. . . . [The articles] frequently point to the capacity of many leaders to overcome obstacles and to elevate their followers to higher levels of commitment. (Bryman 2004: 761)

Daw's (1996) dissertation chapter on leadership provides a thorough review of the major strands of thinking about leadership and highlights how much attention the topic has received.

The flow of words [about leadership] has continued unabated ever since [ancient times], leading Burns to comment that leadership is "one of the most observed and least understood phenomenon on earth.". . . At the publication of his influential tome in 1978 it was still possible for Burns to write that despite an "immense reservoir of data and analyses and theories . . . no central concept or general theory has emerged." (Daw 1996: 13)

Two major spectrums that explain leadership behavior have evolved over the last 100 years: (1) situational leadership versus trait-based leadership and (2) transactional versus transformational leadership. Although both spectrums are similar to one another, there are subtle differences, and these four types of leadership are relevant today.

Situational leaders adapt their leadership style to the situation at hand, reading the characteristics of the situation to determine whether to be authoritarian or consensus-driven, or to use another form of leadership. Transactional leaders use rewards and punishments to elicit the desired behavior to move the organization forward. Pay, time off, bonuses, and other rewards are typical methods of motivation with a transactional leader. In a transactional interaction the leader is promoting a simple exchange. A reward is given for a specific performance. The leader is meeting (and possibly exceeding) the material needs of the followers in return for their cooperation.

Transformational and trait-based leadership have the strongest overlap but are not necessarily a one-to-one match to Abundance Leadership. Both look at the leader's character and traits, but transformational leadership is universally seen as a positive uplifting of employees and organizations to higher-order behaviors.

Transformational leadership, which is (in Burns' original formulation) built on the mutual elevation of the leader and the followers' needs up the scale of Maslow's hierarchy of needs (Maslow, 1954). Both the leader and the led are transformed by the experience. (Daw 1996: 17)

Transformational leaders are often visionary and inspiring or charismatic. Charismatic leaders are those who develop and implement a vision that generates follower enthusiasm by presenting novel ideas or solutions, identifying new opportunities in the environment, delineating a better future for dissatisfied followers, and connecting followers' needs to greater values, goals, or meanings (Cha and Edmondson 2006).

A trait-based leader is not necessarily positive and might use negative traits such as anger to lead and control. These different types of leadership behaviors are not mutually exclusive. A transformational leader can use transactional methods when needed and vice versa.

Recent leadership research has asked more nuanced questions about leadership behavior as well as taking into account the open systems nature of organizations, acknowledging that the leader is one of many elements affecting subordinates' experience and effectiveness. The organizational culture, composed of its history, industry, financing streams, labor market, and more, affects the leader's ability to lead and whether the leader's style will be a good fit with the organization.

Researchers have also become interested in how leadership behaviors and environment interact. Research is moving toward a blended understanding of leadership—trait and situation matter but so do the larger organizational system and context.

The last two fields I explored, economics and sustainability, generate more discussion about scarcity and abundance from a broader vantage point than psychology and organizational development. This broad thinking is a defining trait in Abundance leaders; they want to make the world better.

> Now in the people
> that were meant to be green,
> there is no more life of any kind.
> There is only shriveled barrenness.
>
> The winds are burdened
> by the utterly awful stink of evil,
> selfish goings-on.

Thunderstorms menace.
The air belches out
the filthy uncleanliness of the people.

There pours forth an unnatural,
a loathsome darkness,
that withers the green,
and wizens the fruit
that was to serve as food for the people.

Sometimes this layer of air
is full,
full of a fog that is the source
of many destructive and barren creatures,
that destroy and damage the earth,
rendering it incapable
of sustaining humanity. (Uhlein and St. Hildegard 1984)

Economics and sustainability work at the global level. Economics, since Malthus's chapter on population, has included a strong focus on issues of abundance and scarcity, especially the balance between what has been traditionally defined as progress versus the limitation of the planet's resources to support both human population growth and the growth of per capita consumption (Malthus 1797/1993).

Thomas Robert Malthus's work on population growth was an unintended sentinel piece for the field of sustainability. He posed the fundamental problem for humankind—if we keep growing and using the earth's resources, at some point the population's needs will outstrip the earth's capacity to provide. Since then, many writers and scientists have taken up this essential problem, and it is now a problem that all leaders, especially visionary, Abundance leaders, are called on to address.

The significance of Thomas Robert Malthus' work was not in his solution to the problem of natural resource scarcity, but in the manner that he framed the problem. Because Malthus discussed the dynamics of population growth and the limitations of the earth's resources, social scientists had to acknowledge that the

*problem of mankind's survival on a fixed, limited, and delicate
environmental base was critical, particularly in view of the
growing population and expanding industry. (Finnin and
Smith 1979: 108)*

The concept of sustainability was created to meet this challenge.
Sustainability is focused on the earth's capacity to meet the needs of
human beings without destroying the delicate balance and interactions
that keep the earth's ecosystem functioning, while sustaining the quality
of choices for future generations. In the late 1950s and early 1960s,
economists, and then environmentalists and others, turned their attention to understanding, proving, and discussing Malthus's work. One of
the primary catalysts of this revived and heated dialogue was Rachel
Carson's 1962 book, *Silent Spring*.

The clear decline in the quality and quantity of the world's natural
resources continues to push theorists to examine the implications of
human consumption and economics. William M. Finnin and Gerald A.
Smith (1979) write, "To the Malthusian all solutions will eventually
require a less wasteful, more rational use of our finite resources" (3).
Also in *The Morality of Scarcity*, a collection of lectures given in 1976–
1977, the topics on scarcity range from the American health care system
to foreign policy, covering a wide range of human activities.

Once the concern about achieving a dynamic and sustainable global
balance took root in the sciences, the very definition of progress was and
continues to be called into question. As mentioned at the start of this
section, defining progress is of deep concern to Abundance leaders who
grapple with questions such as these:

- What constitutes abundance?
- What constitutes progress and when is enough enough?
- How can I and my organization make things better?

Bookchin (1971) makes a lengthy but eloquent argument for a new
conception of progress, questioning capitalism's materialism and its negative effect on individuals and communities.

*For one thing, scarcity is more than a condition of scarce
resources: the word, if it is to mean anything in human terms,*

must encompass the social relations and cultural apparatus that foster insecurity in the psyche. In organic societies this insecurity may be a function of the oppressive limits established by a precarious natural world; in a hierarchical society it is a function of the repressive limits established by an exploitative class structure. By the same token, the word "post-scarcity" means fundamentally more than a mere abundance of the means of life: it decidedly includes the kind of life these means support. The human relationships and psyche of the individual in a post-scarcity society must fully reflect the freedom, security and self-expression that this abundance makes possible. Post-scarcity society, in short, is the fulfillment of the social and cultural potentialities latent in a technology of abundance. (11)

Here Bookchin is arguing that a post-scarcity society is not about having more material goods, but about using our technological advances to create a quality of life (psychological, communal, spiritual) that is abundant.

There is an alternative view of economic abundance, seen less in the academic environment and more so in popular literature, that suggests that material abundance is inherently good and overlooks the high cost of excessive abundance to the planet and human culture. One such example is a brief article by John Keeble (2001), a financial planner:

The abundance mentality holds that wealth is being created all the time by free people who are highly motivated. Whenever a person achieves or acquires something, it causes more wealth and more prosperity for more people. The free enterprise system of the United States has generated more wealth and abundance for more people than any system in history and has created the best system for distributing it fairly, although that system certainly can and should be improved. (Abstract)

There are several problems with this argument. First is a naiveté about the fairness of the US system of distribution, which has been called into question by hundreds of writers and researchers ranging from Malcolm X (X and Haley 1973) to Jonathan Kozol (1991).

Another problem with Keeble's definition is an unawareness of the corollary social costs of material abundance. When a culture has grown accustomed to having all its wants (versus needs) filled, to wanting more than it needs, and to learning to have new wants met on a regular basis, the end result is degradation of the system's sustainability.

There is also a real human cost to many of the means of production. Unregulated factories with child labor or harsh conditions in less developed countries that produce the goods for more developed countries have a real cost for all of us. In addition, the disposable trinkets, like those given out by McDonald's to children, ultimately end up degrading the environment in landfills around the country.

Keeble's work so clearly highlights the importance of defining *enough* for an individual. If *enough* is dramatically more than a person needs and is gained through systems that damage the ecology, then *enough* can only result in degradation of the environment, the ultimate system in which we all operate.

Overall, economists and sustainability theorists, as well as organizational leaders, are now struggling with ways to manage the impact of capitalism, industrialism, and materialism. Fricker (1998) says,

> *Stripped of its finery economics is about how we exchange our surpluses, whereas as a science it has somehow been transformed into an economics of scarcity where everything is expressed in monetary terms. . . . The third party to an economic transaction is the earth, the Great Mother . . . We have created the shadow of scarcity, the polar shadow of which is greed. This is fuelled by the dominant world mental model based on rationality and self-interest. We have conveniently forgotten the paradox of coopera-tion.* Rational, self-interested individuals will not act to achieve the common or group interests. *Fortunately we are not always rational and will cooperate when we really come to know and trust each other and have the power and resources to implement solutions. This is a foundation to an economics of abundance—of labour, goodwill, and renewable resources, even though the lat-ter now occupies a tenuous position. Alternative world views are emerging to facilitate the change in mind set, from George Soros through Richard Douthwaite to Ken Wilber. (Abstract)*

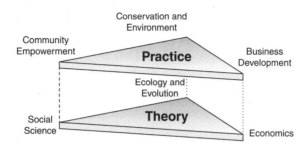

FIGURE 2.2   Relationship of practice to theory in sustainability.

SOURCE: Gunderson et al, 2001 / Island Press.

Other theorists echo this call to integrate theories and practice to move toward real change.

> *It is quite clear that actions are firmly, if subliminally, grounded in theories of ecology and evolution, economics and free markets, and social and institutional dynamics. These theories have been developed in separate disciplines with distinctive habits of mind. Each set of theories can point to remarkable successes within its own domain. Each set of theories is necessary, yet insufficient, to develop a theory of sustainability. Academics encounter many incentives to maintain the purity of the disciplines, and few incentives for integration, yet integration is essential to solve the sustainability problem. (Gunderson and Holling 2001: 124) (See Figure 2.2.)*

Paul Hawken's (1993) clear and cogent work, *The Ecology of Commerce*, represents a powerful synthesis of ecology and economics through a sustainability lens. It is a clear response to Malthus's challenge, and to some extent the challenge posed by Marx and Engels (Tucker 1972). Hawken's (1993) writing has the wonderful and rare mix of depth, elegance, and accessibility. Without bashing free market economies wholesale, Hawken articulates the problems that have arisen over the previous century as a result of those economies and calls us to rethink our core definitions of success.

His work begins with a laying out of the problem. "We have reached an unsettling and portentous turning point in industrial civilization" (Hawken 1993: 1). Hawken lays out the usual grim statistics of industry's impact on the earth's ecosystem, which have only worsened since he wrote in 1993:

> *5.5 billion people are breeding exponentially.. . . We know we have decimated ninety-seven percent of the ancient forests in North America; the Ogalala Aquifer . . . will dry up within thirty to forty years at present rates of extraction . . . Businesspeople must either dedicate themselves to transforming commerce to a restorative undertaking, or march society to the undertaker. (xi)*

He argues that corporations are the dominant form of organization on the planet and so we must fundamentally rethink what the purpose of business is. In the very first chapter he lays out a quiet but powerful vision for what business could accomplish.

> *The promise of business is not, or should not be, simply to make money. Nor is it merely a system of making and selling things. The promise of business is to increase the general well-being of humankind through service, a creative invention and ethical philosophy. (1)*

Hawken (1993) notes that "rather than a management problem, we have a design problem, a flaw that runs through all business" (xiii). This is a helpful perspective for leaders. He points out that most businesses are designed to maximize profits without taking into account the real costs to the environment and society as a whole.

> *To create an enduring society, we will need a system of commerce and production where each and every act is inherently sustainable and restorative. Business will need to integrate economic, biologic, and human systems to create a sustainable method of commerce. (xiv)*

He proposes a fundamental mental model shift where "more and faster" are not the measurements of organizational success. Restorative and in balance become the guides.

Hawken (1993) is above all practical and concrete and to that end he proposes eight objectives, which Abundance leaders can adapt and apply:

1. *Reduce absolute consumption of energy and natural resources in the North by 80% within the next half century.*
2. *Provide secure, stable, and meaningful employment for people everywhere.*
3. *Be self-actuating as opposed to regulated or morally mandated.*
4. *Honor market principles.*
5. *Be more rewarding than our present way of life.*
6. *Exceed sustainability by restoring degraded habitats and ecosystems to their fullest biological capacity.*
7. *Rely on current income.*
8. *Be fun and engaging. (xiv–xvi)*

In the final analysis, Hawken asks us to rethink our underlying mental models about business, about wants and needs, and about success.

John Adams's (2000) work, *Thinking Today as if Tomorrow Mattered*, is an excellent complement to Hawken's work. Adams enhances the spiritual elements of Hawken's work and suggests that a deeper consciousness, a new consciousness, is required. He first echoes Hawken's call for organizations and individuals to take action.

> *And today, financial enterprise has become the dominant institution all over the world. The church took responsibility when it was dominant; the state took responsibility when it was dominant, and now there is really nobody taking responsibility for the whole, which is now the eco-system of the planet. (98)*

Adams (2000) then takes the systems view of the situation. He notes that it is normal in a system for extreme views to appear before a breakthrough to a new way of thinking and being takes hold. "As environmentalist groups become stronger and more vocal, so too do militia groups. . . . Behavior patterns seem to be polarizing and becoming more extreme in every walk of life" (156). In these extremes, Adams, clearly an optimist, sees "the seeds of a successful way ahead."

Adams (2000), based on the work of Paul Ray, Ken Wilber, and even Einstein, argues that a new group of people, the "Cultural Creatives" (158), are emerging and will help take the planet in a whole new direction. According to Ray (1996), this kind of sea change occurs only once or twice every 1,000 years. This group of people will help design and introduce a new way of structuring our economy and our interaction with the planet. Ray's Cultural Creatives have a parallel in Richard Dawkins's (1990) memes. Memes are ideas that move through and change a culture, similar to physical characteristics that survive and spread through generations of a species.

Economics and sustainability offer innumerable examples of scarcity and abundance ideas, issues, and system characteristics. The field's underlying dilemma, so beautifully articulated in Malthus's chapter more than 200 years ago, has not been solved. It is more completely understood; yet, the movement toward a recovered environment, not just the sustaining of the currently degraded environment, has barely begun. The field of sustainability calls into question the fundamental architecture of our social systems and economic structures such as capitalism.

There is an elegant and important connection between the world's need to shift core mental models and structures and the leader's need to do the same in the microcosm of their organization. If sustainable abundance mental models are inherently healthier for the organization and its staff members, how does abundance avoid degrading the ecosystems in which the organization operates? Is a leadership mental model of sustainability a better base for leadership behaviors?

The Abundance Leadership model encourages leaders to rethink the underlying structures of the economy, their organizations, and the effect of both on the planet's gorgeous and fragile ecosystem.

CHAPTER **3**

Four Meta-Competencies

Our business in life is not to get ahead of others, but to get ahead of ourselves.

—E. JOSEPH COSSMAN

Abundance Leadership is a great model for leaders who are open to vision and expansion. It is a concept that is not commonly considered in this work world. Generally speaking, we approach work (and life) from a context of what isn't working and what has to be corrected. Abundance Leadership comes from a context of positivity and abundance. That very simple approach says quite a bit about the power and value of this concept.

—ABUNDANCE LEADERSHIP IMMERSION PROGRAM ALUMNI

In this chapter, I begin to explore the meta-competencies of an Abundance leader, which are the overarching skills and habits of such a leader. In Section III of this book, I provide a detailed how-to manual that give tips and techniques for manifesting more abundance behaviors.

The four meta-competencies are visioning, visibility, self-awareness, and managing well. Each one has competencies, of which there are 11 total. Each competency, in turn, has its own behaviors, of which there are a total of 29 reflecting abundance and 27 reflecting scarcity.

Table 3.1 shows how abundance behaviors map to each competency and meta-competency. Scarcity behaviors are listed after the table. Notice that some abundance behaviors can have a negative impact. Anything in excess is problematic.

There are a few seemingly odd or incongruent abundance behaviors in this list: "takes chances and gets overburdened easily" and "lacks focus and can be recklessly optimistic." My original research showed that these two

TABLE 3.1   The Abundance Leadership Competencies

Meta-Competency	Competency	Abundance Behavior
Visioning	Visioning	Has a compelling vision that they are able to communicate and on which they build their organization
		Builds on the past but is not constrained by it
		Thinks in the long term and the big picture
		Exudes and conveys energy and hope for good outcomes
		Focuses on the bottom line—is financially savvy
	Creativity	Seeks creative and alternative ways of solving problems
		Has high technical expertise
		Has high cognitive intelligence
Visibility	Visibility	Manages by walking around; is visible to staff members
		Does not hide in their office; maximizes contact with others
Self-Awareness	Reflection and affect	Seeks out the opinion and energy of others when appropriate
		Is rarely ruffled and keeps an even tone and affect in most situations
		Manages their time well
	Interpersonal adeptness	Demonstrates empathy and compassion for others
		Gives their attention and kindness without effort
		Addresses conflict
	Morality	Has a strong moral compass that is evident in their language and actions
		Is trustworthy
	Ego control	Is humble
		Is not egocentric; does not have a "me, me" attitude

Meta-Competency	Competency	Abundance Behavior
Managing Well	Team building	Looks for opportunities to build teams
		Understands and articulates the role others play in the success of the team
		Delegates
		Guides and challenges employees so that they develop
	Communication	Proactively shares as much information as possible
		Seeks out feedback and receives it with openness; willingly learns from mistakes
	Protection	Protects staff members from abusive conditions
		Seeks out resources and is able to gain resources for their staff members
		Maintains healthy organizational and psychological boundaries for themselves and their team°
	Decision-making	Is decisive
		Does not make inappropriately dictatorial decisions

°This behavior is not part of the original research and has been added as the model has been applied.

behaviors are seen by the research participants as abundance behaviors, but obviously ones that an Abundance leader wants to moderate or avoid.

Scarcity behaviors include the following:

- Has low emotional or social intelligence
- Escalates disagreements fast
- Tolerates substandard performance
- Doesn't take time to celebrate successes
- Does not encourage a work–life balance
- Does not advocate for their employees
- Does not do much in the way of coaching and developing their employees
- Is easily offended but also prone to give offense easily
- Hides in their office; minimizes contact with others
- Avoids conflict

- Controls communication and discourages contact between others
- Makes dictatorial decisions
- Doesn't delegate and micromanages others
- Is calculating and manipulative
- Is untrustworthy
- Blames others
- Is suspicious
- Is lazy
- Is physically and verbally unsettled, easily angered, and appears rattled
- Is egocentric; has a me, me, me attitude
- Lacks vision and has a myopic view of the future
- Has a negative view of others; sees people as having limited ability and tends to mistrust others
- Abuses power
- Openly favors certain employees by giving the same people plum work or projects
- Settles for old ways of doing things, without questioning protocol
- Hoards information
- Acts out of fear; is fearful
- Talks down to people; is condescending

Another important finding of my research was what I refer to as *signal behaviors*. Out of the 56 behaviors, some had higher correlations than others to people's perceptions of someone as either an Abundance leader or a Scarcity leader. These signal behaviors are the brightest cues to your staff members about your mental model. Abundance signal behaviors include these:

- Guides and challenges employees so they develop
- Looks for opportunities to build teams
- Understands and articulates the role others play in the success of the team
- Proactively shares as much information as possible
- Seeks creative and alternative ways of solving problems

Scarcity signal behaviors include these:

- Talks down to people; is condescending
- Controls communication and discourages contact between others

- Hoards information
- Abuses power
- Blames others

The model can help you determine where on the spectrum of abundance-scarcity mental models you are, and which behaviors related to this spectrum you can change to be a more effective leader.

In the research, bosses were easily identified as a scarcity, abundance, or mixed-model boss. In general, bosses with an abundance paradigm—seeing the world as resource sufficient and power as shareable—are preferred over scarcity bosses, and they have healthier organizations to show for it. Their organizations resolve conflict better, have better communication patterns, and better teamwork. There is a caveat here: too much abundance can be detrimental by dispersing energy, losing focus, and misplaced optimism. Scarcity bosses are more difficult to work for and negatively affect their organization's perceived health. Subordinates did not unilaterally dislike working for scarcity bosses, but it was hard to find a subordinate who liked their scarcity boss.

In every organization staff members work in an ecosystem of energy that grows, shrinks, sheers away, encourages greatness, and even causes pain. Each individual's contribution and behavior affect the organization's ecosystem of energy. When an organization's ecosystem is in right relationship with all of its elements (staff members, customers, vendors, and more), the organization also positively affects the larger community and planet.

It is the particular mandate of leaders and managers to attend to their organization's ecosystem of energy on a tireless basis to realize the organization's purpose and have a positive impact on the world. Managing and leading start with high self-awareness, followed by artful ways of engaging people and groups, all wrapped in a passionate, centered, Abundance Leadership paradigm that is manifested daily.

The Abundance Leadership model asks the fundamental question: in the leader's mind, are there enough resources (time, money, power, compassion, and more) so that the leader is magnanimous with their energy, attention, and power, in turn creating energy and enthusiasm in their subordinates?

Let's look at an overview of each of the four meta-competencies: visioning, visibility, self-awareness, and managing well.

VISIONING FOR THE GREATER GOOD

We are looking ahead, as is one of the first mandates
given us as chiefs, to make sure that every decision that
we make relates to the welfare and well-being of the
seventh generation to come. . . . What about the seventh
generation? Where are you taking them? What will
they have?

—OREN LYONS, CHIEF OF THE ONONDAGA NATION

The future depends on what you do today.

—MAHATMA GANDHI

Enthusiasm for a meaningful, better future is contagious.

—SOURCE UNKNOWN

The underlying abundance belief is that there is enough for all, and
that excessive accumulation of wealth and resources hurts others and the
planet in the long run. Having enough is good enough. My son once
asked me, "Are we rich?" My response was, "We have more than we
need, so yes we are."

Abundance leaders want their organizations to have a positive impact
on their staff members, their community, and the world. I believe that,
in the current political and economic system we have in the United
States, organizations serve as a primary cultural driver and moral barom-
eter, partially because right now our government system is not working
well. It will work well again (I'm an optimist) and it has worked well in
the past. If we make some systemic changes to our government, it will
work even better in the future.

In the meantime, organizations, for-profit and nonprofit, are driving
culture, and they are driving people's daily experiences. I want to encourage you as a leader to think about your organization as a microcosm of
what is possible. Instead of patching and layering actions on a badly built
organizational chassis (e.g., putting policies one over the other, or working
on only one part of a systemic issue such as gender equity by saying, "Let's
just look at compensation. If we solve compensation, then we've got

gender equity"), I encourage you to tackle societal issues through your organization's policies, which are de facto issues for your organization.

Abundance leaders understand that the decisions they make about their organization have ripple effects out to the staff members' families and community. Abundance leaders want to use the time and energy of their organization to make the world better; they understand that they have the opportunity to make decisions about how resources are used that will change lives.

"The world we inhabit is abundant beyond our wildest imagination. There are trees, dreams, sunrises; there are thunderstorms, shadows, rivers; there are wars, flea bites, love affairs; there are the lives of people, God, entire galaxies."

—*Paul Feyerabend (Feyerabend and Terpstra 1999: 5)*

At OPG, we do many things throughout the year to enact our mission. "OPG's mission is to create a better world—one rich with a spirit of abundance, innovation, compassion, and respect. Our work is designed to facilitate deep human connections that form the basis of thriving workplaces and communities. Using our own office as a laboratory, we work alongside our clients to create extraordinary work cultures and to build momentum toward our common goal of a better world."

Visionary leaders—leaders for the 21st century, for the millennium—need to change their own organizations, activating the energy of their internal cultures to achieve results for all 4 Ps (planet, people, profit, and purpose). Here are examples of leaders who are using their position to make bold promises and are changing the world for the better.

Hamdi Ulukaya, Chobani

Hamdi Ulukaya (Figure 3.1) is the founder and CEO of Chobani, America's second largest yogurt maker. "Ulukaya gives much of the credit for Chobani's meteoric growth to his adherence to what he has called the 'anti-CEO playbook.' Instead of emphasizing maximizing shareholder returns (what Ulukaya has called 'the dumbest idea I've heard of in my life'), his anti-CEO playbook emphasizes taking care of employees first, helping the communities in which you operate, having

FIGURE 3.1   Hamdi Ulukaya, founder of Chobani.
SOURCE: Michael Gonda/Wikimedia Commons.

the courage to take positions on social issues and being extremely accountable to consumers" (Hessekiel 2022).

His progressive leadership includes the following foci:

1. *Seeking opportunities to hire immigrants and refugees and providing them with support to succeed such as extra training and transportation.*
2. *Focus on a mission of creating "better food for more people" even if that requires extra investment in products that detracts from short-term profits.*
3. *Moving quickly and generously to contribute huge quantities of yogurt to help nourish people during the pandemic.*

Ulukaya expressed great confidence that these and other pro-social moves benefit society and the company. "In the long term, you always get the reward for doing things right," he said. It has never been more important than at this challenging time for businesses like Chobani "to fix any injustices we see in the world" (Hessekiel 2022).

FIGURE 3.2   Ed Bastian, CEO of Delta Airlines.

SOURCE: AP images/Curtis Compton/Atlanta Journal-Constitution.

Ed Bastian, Delta Airlines

"CEO Ed Bastian [Figure 3.2] told CNBC on Friday the company is going 'fully carbon neutral' starting March 1. 'It's a big challenge and it's a big commitment,' Bastian said on Squawk Box. Delta is committing at least $1 billion over the next decade to reduce environmental impact, focusing on clean technological investments for engines and carbon removal, he added. 'There's no greater challenge that I know of that we need to be investing in and innovating in as environmental sustainability,' he said" (Bursztynsky 2020).

Whitney Wolfe Herd, Bumble

"Instead of sitting back when faced with sexual harassment, Whitney Wolfe [Figure 3.3] stood up and gave women the power. Wolfe left her role as vice president of marketing at Tinder due to a sexual harassment

FIGURE 3.3   Whiney Wolfe Herd, founder of Bumble.

SOURCE: Jerod Harris/Getty Images/Entertainment/Getty Images.

and discrimination lawsuit and started Bumble, a dating app where the women get to make the first move and where harassment is strictly policed. Bumble is now the second most popular dating app and worth billions of dollars. In 2021, Bumble went public, making Wolfe Herd the youngest woman to take a company public and the world's youngest female self-made billionaire. Wolfe Herd frequently speaks to and mentors other female entrepreneurs, and under her leadership, an amazing 70% of Bumble's board is women" (Morgan 2021).

Maria Eitel, Nike Foundation and Girl Effect

"Maria Eitel [Figure 3.4] spent the early days of her career working for the White House and Microsoft before joining Nike as the company's first vice president of corporate responsibility. In 2004, she founded the Nike Foundation and created the theory of The Girl Effect—the idea that adolescent girls have a unique ability to stop poverty before it starts. [She founded] Girl Effect, an organization with a goal of helping 250 million young girls below the poverty line in four key areas: ending early marriage and delaying first birth, enhancing the health and safety of girls, increasing secondary school completion and improving access to economic assets. Her work has already helped millions of girls around the world and is only getting started" (Center for Management & Organization Effectiveness 2022).

FIGURE 3.4   Marie Eitel.

SOURCE: Russell Watkins/DFID—UK Department for International Development.

Jacinda Ardern, Prime Minister of New Zealand

Before her resignation, Jacinda Ardern commented on the difficulty of leading a country as a young mother, but noted how those skills helped her lead.

"Leading a country is hard enough—but try doing it as a new mother. When she was elected Prime Minister of New Zealand in 2017 at age 37, Jacinda Ardern [Figure 3.5] was the world's youngest female head of state. Less than a year into her term, she gave birth to her first daughter, and has since even given major speeches with her daughter on her lap. Tapping into her maternal instincts and femininity have helped Arden lead causes like unity and social change. At the same time, Ardern has taken quick and decisive action against gun violence. Her strong leadership during the pandemic led to only 25 New Zealanders dying from the virus" (Center for Management & Organization Effectiveness 2022).

FIGURE 3.5   Jacinda Ardern, prime minister of New Zealand.

SOURCE: Dave Rowland/Getty Images/News/Getty Images.

Warren Buffett

Warren Buffett (Figure 3.6) is one of the most successful investors in the world. He is currently the CEO of Berkshire Hathaway. He has also pledged to give away nearly 99% of his accumulated wealth to philanthropic causes after his death (Center for Management & Organization Effectiveness 2022).

One of the challenges I see in some of the leaders of our client organizations, including Abundance leaders who are just beginning to

FIGURE 3.6   Warren Buffet, CEO of Berkshire Hathaway.

SOURCE: Abaca Press/Alamy Stock Photo.

formulate big ideas for their companies, is that they can be prone to buying into the marketplace's current structure, limitations, and guiding principles. For example, they rationalize away the undervaluing of "women's work" or the pink collar professions (teaching, nursing, caregivers) with statements such as, "But that's fair market pay." This is not inspirational leadership. This type of leadership perpetuates a status quo that hurts individuals, organizations, and our society.

As mentioned in Chapter 2, you might consider using Paul Hawken's eight-point "manifesto" as a starting point.

1. *Reduce absolute consumption of energy and natural resources in the North by 80% within the next half century.*
2. *Provide secure, stable, and meaningful employment for people everywhere.*
3. *Be self-actuating as opposed to regulated or morally mandated.*
4. *Honor market principles.*
5. *Be more rewarding than our present way of life.*

6. *Exceed sustainability by restoring degraded habitats and ecosystems to their fullest biological capacity.*
7. *Rely on current income.*
8. *Be fun and engaging. (xiv–xvi)*

We have looked at the value of having an abundance orientation and the power that organizational leaders have to change the world. The other three Abundance Leadership meta-competencies help bring this power to life.

VISIBILITY

It is important for staff members and other key constituents to see you regularly. Because of your iconic status as leader, your presence and visibility provides reassurance that there is someone at the helm, that you are accessible, and that you are functioning. It sounds strange to mention the last but it is important for people to know that you are healthy and functioning and capable of leading. These subconscious and conscious needs of your constituents are true also for your leadership team that surrounds you. Steve Keating articulates the power of being visible:

> *But one [leadership] characteristic is seldom mentioned. That characteristic is being visible. If your people can't see you then your people can't follow you.*
>
> *As a leader you are the model for the culture of your organization. You are the face of the values your organization represents. You are the cheerleader in chief and the light of hope when circumstances look dark. But you can't be any of those things if you're not seen . . . on a very regular basis.*
>
> *There are many ways to communicate with your people these days. You can write a company blog. You can publish a weekly video. You can do email blasts a few times a week. But none of those can come close to just being "out there" among the people you lead. Short hallway conversations with anyone and everyone in your organization makes everyone feel as if they belong. The higher up you are in the organization the more these brief conversations are valued by the people you lead.*

*And there's the challenge. The higher you are in the organi-
zation the more likely you are to get bogged down with the day-
to-day requirements of managing the organization. It may feel as
if the last thing you have time for is a talk with Patty from the
mail room or Jerry from the loading dock. You may not even
have time to talk with all your senior leaders.*

But that's a terrible mistake.

*If you're wondering about how to tell if you're "out there"
frequently enough, here is the only measurement that counts.
The measurement is your people's opinion. If your people think
you're invisible then you are. If they never see you then you
might as well not exist. You can tell yourself that you're more
than visible but you don't get a vote. The perception of your people is all that matters. (Keating 2022)*

Depending on the size of your organization, you can be visible in a
variety of ways. There is the physical visibility of walking around. The
old idea of managing by walking around (**MBWA**) is still a valid and useful tool as a leader. The size of your organization will dictate how much
you can use this tool. When I was the director of OD at Yale, I had
about 27 staff members on two floors. Every morning, whenever I
could, I would stop and chat with each staff member, sometimes in
small groups. I'm an extrovert so I loved making the connection with
the staff members and hearing what they were working on and how I
might be helpful.

There are many more modern, high-tech ways to be visible.
Teleconferencing has been a game changer. Large town halls broadcast
across the globe can work also. Reaching out weekly with an update to
your staff members, written in your voice, can be very effective as well.

The key with visibility as a meta-competency is to pay attention to
the frequency with which you are being visible and providing access to
the whole range of constituents and groups within your organization. It
doesn't hurt to keep an organizational map handy at your desk. Take a
look at it regularly and ask how and when have I been in contact with
each group? What information might they be seeking in order to do
their jobs better and to feel reassured about our progress as an
organization?

SELF-AWARENESS

*There are two overarching personal capabilities that help lead-
ers "learn how to learn" new skills and competencies: self-
awareness (or identity) and adaptability. (Hall 2004)*

My ex-husband, Brett Rayford, with whom I teach and consult occa-
sionally, is a licensed psychologist. He would sometimes say about someone that we had encountered, "They have no appreciation for their
affect." I've always loved that phrase to describe people who are una-
ware of how they come off to others, which is most of us! Self-awareness
can help solve this problem to some extent. K. Mansas Showry makes a
powerful argument for exploring your inner life and reflecting on your
experiences:

*Many theories and thinkers have attempted to explore what truly
makes a person emerge as a leader. Successful leadership often
surfaces when people become aware of critical personal experiences in their life, understand the driving forces, respond by
rethinking about self, redirect their moves and reshape their
actions. Stanford [Graduate School of Business] rates soft skills
like self-awareness as one of the pillars of managerial capabilities
that predicts managerial effectiveness and leadership success.*

*It suggests that IQ and technical skills are far less important
to leadership success than self-awareness. In a world of unprec-
edented business complexities, leaders, besides explicit knowledge, need an inner compass of self-awareness to walk the tight
rope of leadership. (Showry 2014)*

When I start a coaching engagement with a client, I will ask them if
they have ever done therapy or counseling of any kind. If they say no, it
raises concerns for me. I am worried that they have not explored in
depth the things that trigger them, the things that give them joy, the way
they come off to other people, and other deep explorations of behaviors
and drivers that make them who they are.

I want to be clear here. This exploration of the self is not always or
completely about changing yourself to suit others. I would argue that it

is discovering who you are and with whom you can best work, as well as discovering how to adapt or refine your behaviors so they produce even more positive results and a more positive impact in the world. "As leaders strive for excellence, self-efficacy and self-awareness can empower them to unlock their own potential and the potential of their organizations and those with whom they work" (Caldwell and Hayes 2016).

Self-awareness and internal growth take time and effort and are ongoing activities, just as is organizational development (OD) for any company. We don't start on a path to self-awareness and then say at some point we've achieved it 100%. We might take breaks from the exploration, but we need to come back to it at regular intervals to continue to grow as leaders, partners, parents, and even as children to our elderly parents.

I tell my coaching clients and my leadership clients: don't rush or strive for perfection. We are only perfect at two moments in our life. At our first breath. And at our last breath. If we strive for perfection, we are striving for the end. Let us strive for better.

OD work is the organizational equivalent of individual self-awareness work. OD is the continual examining of an organization's culture, infrastructure, policies, team habits, and more in the service of creating a continually growing and improving organization.

OD is not a technique or a group of tools, though some OD professionals practice as if it were. Rather, OD can be applied any time an organization wants to make planned improvements using the OD values. OD might be used in any of the following situations:

➤ *To develop or enhance the organization's mission statement (statement of purpose) or vision statement for what it wants to be*
➤ *To help align functional structures in an organization so they are working together for a common purpose*
➤ *To create a strategic plan for how the organization is going to make decisions about its future and achieving that future*
➤ *To manage conflict that exists among individuals, groups, functions, sites, and so on when such conflicts disrupt the ability of the organization to function in a healthy way*

> ➤ *To put in place processes that will help improve the ongoing operations of the organization on a continuous basis*
> ➤ *To create a collaborative environment that helps the organization be more effective and efficient*
> ➤ *To create reward systems that are compatible with the goals of the organization*
> ➤ *To assist in the development of policies and procedures that will improve the ongoing operation of the organization*
> ➤ *To assess the working environment, to identify strengths on which to build and areas in which change and improvement are needed*
> ➤ *To provide help and support for employees, especially those in senior positions, who need an opportunity to be coached in how to do their jobs better*
> ➤ *To assist in creating systems for providing feedback on individual performance and, on occasion, conducting studies to give individuals feedback and coaching to help them in their individual development (Marshall 2017)*

MANAGING WELL

Managing well is the last of the four meta-competencies on which all abundance leaders focus. Managing well requires using a deep and wide toolkit. In that toolkit, we find everything from how a leader interacts one-on-one with staff members to how they think about policies and procedures.

If you started your career in a particular profession such as accounting or medicine or architecture, the odds are high that you never received management training, or maybe you've received a little bit here and there. Give yourself permission to study and learn how to manage. Find people inside and outside your organization with whom you can discuss different management techniques and how to implement them. You will make mistakes along the way, and you will adjust and adapt. But managing well is an important ongoing pursuit.

> *[T]here is one quality that sets truly great managers apart from the rest: They discover what is unique about each person and*

then capitalize on it. Average managers play checkers, while great managers play chess. The difference? In checkers, all the pieces are uniform and move in the same way; they are interchangeable. You need to plan and coordinate their movements, certainly, but they all move at the same pace, on parallel paths. In chess, each type of piece moves in a different way, and you can't play if you don't know how each piece moves. More important, you won't win if you don't think carefully about how you move the pieces. Great managers know and value the unique abilities and even the eccentricities of their employees, and they learn how best to integrate them into a coordinated plan of attack.

This is the exact opposite of what great leaders do. Great leaders discover what is universal and capitalize on it. Their job is to rally people toward a better future. Leaders can succeed in this only when they can cut through differences of race, sex, age, nationality, and personality and, using stories and celebrating heroes, tap into those very few needs we all share. The job of a manager, meanwhile, is to turn one person's particular talent into performance. Managers will succeed only when they can identify and deploy the differences among people, challenging each employee to excel in his or her own way. This doesn't mean a leader can't be a manager or vice versa. But to excel at one or both, you must be aware of the very different skills each role requires. (Buckingham 2005)

In the Abundance Leadership model, the following management skills are paramount:

- ➤ Team building
  - ○ Looks for opportunities to build teams
  - ○ Understands and articulates the role others play in the success of the team
  - ○ Guides and challenges employees so that they develop
- ➤ Communication
  - ○ Proactively shares as much information as possible
  - ○ Seeks out feedback and receives it with openness, and willingly learns from mistakes

- Protection
  - Protects staff members from abusive conditions
  - Seeks out resources and is able to gain resources for their staff members
- Decision-making
  - Manages their time well

Staff members always appreciate a manager who is working to become a better manager. If you find in your leadership journey that you are better at managing some types of employees rather than others, or direct management is not your forte, consider surrounding yourself with a leadership team that is good at managing.

In my consulting practice I have advised on numerous occasions that organizations hire both a content or visionary leader as well as a practical managing leader. In the theater industry, this often manifests in the organizational chart as an artistic director and a managing director. Or it might be an executive director and a managing director. In the private sector, the titles might be chief executive officer and chief operating officer.

Building on the work of self-awareness, I encourage you to design your leadership position and leadership team in a way that enables you to be the best you can be in your role.

SECTION

Organizational Health and Abundance Leadership

Organizational health is the single greatest competitive advantage in any business.

—Patrick Lencioni

Abundance leaders have healthier organizations. The research that created the Abundance Leadership model produced a valid and reliable measure of organizational health. In this section we will look at that measure and discuss ways to help your organization sustain and improve its health.

CHAPTER **4**

Improving Your Organization's Health

The first wealth is health.

—RALPH WALDO EMERSON

It is not sufficient to be an admired leader. Results matter, and robust and resilient organizational health is critical for producing those results. My research showed that an optimistic or abundance mental model does matter in a leader. That mental model has a positive impact on individuals working for such a boss, and it makes for a healthier organization. A healthy organization is often more effective, whether measured in profitability or service delivery, and is often an asset to the larger community by creating more satisfied and productive staff.

According to the organizational health measure (OHM) I created during my doctoral research, a healthy organization has better communication, conflict resolution, teamwork, supervision, and other characteristics. The OHM provides a meaningful and useful tool for practitioners to measure the perceived health of an organization. It can be contrasted and enhanced with more quantitative measures such as data from balance sheets or income statements to see if perceived health and financial health coexist.

This provides a reason to care about abundance and scarcity behaviors. If the behaviors had no impact on the organization, why bother studying and practicing them? Given the direct correlation, bosses are well-served to determine their scarcity or abundance tendencies and to work on managing those toward a more abundance model.

You know intuitively whether the place you work is fundamentally healthy and thriving or is suffering from "chronic illnesses" or "emergency trauma." What clues is your intuition picking up on? Here are five to consider:

> A turnover rate that seems out of the ordinary for the industry or the economic times. At OPG our turnover rate is high for staff in their first year; however, it is in line with the management consulting industry.
> Cattiness and pettiness among staff members runs rampant; there are whispers in the hallways and unresolved conflict.
> The humor has gone out of the place; there's no fun happening anywhere.
> The leadership is nonexistent or detrimental to the organization.
> Finances are tight or in decline in ways that can't be explained by an investment strategy or economic circumstances.

The OHM has 20 attributes that determine an organization's health:

> <u>Communication in the organization</u>. Is it effective the majority of the time?
> <u>Conflict resolution</u>. How well is conflict addressed?
> <u>Sense of hierarchy</u>. How appropriately hierarchical is the organization?
> <u>Teamwork and camaraderie</u>. Do teams get work done and do people have a sense of camaraderie?
> <u>Timeliness of decision-making</u>. Are decisions made in a timely manner?
> <u>Decision-making processes</u>. Are decisions made in a variety of ways, each appropriate to the problem being solved?
> <u>Supervision and management of employees</u>. Are there robust supervision and management standards, expectations, expertise, and systems?
> <u>Responsibility and accountability of people</u> in the organization to their work and to each other. Do people do their work in a timely manner and do they hold each other accountable?
> <u>Information flow</u>. Does information flow in a timely manner and is enough information shared?
> <u>Productivity</u>. Are people generally productive in the organization?
> <u>Promotion</u>. Are people promoted from within in a reasonable time frame?

- ➤ Creativity. Is the organization creative and does it encourage creativity in its staff members?
- ➤ Appropriate use of power. Do people in the organization use their power appropriately without abusing it?
- ➤ Leadership's energy. Does the leadership have enthusiasm and energy for the task of leading (versus being burned out)?
- ➤ Empowerment of lower-level employees. Are lower-level employees engaged in the important conversations and do they have truly effective means for making changes, resolving concerns, and participating in the life of the organization?
- ➤ Dealing with failure in a positive, nonpunitive way. How is failure handled? Do people learn and grow or are people fired or demoted?
- ➤ Morale. Is morale in the organization high, with people feeling generally positive about work?
- ➤ Development and support of employees. Are there clear opportunities, programs, and/or funds for the development of employees?
- ➤ Policies, procedures, and processes are supportive and appropriate for the work of the organization.
- ➤ Financial health. Is the organization financially viable? Financial health is usually considered a prerequisite for all other health measures—without financial health, the measures identified here are irrelevant.

The last two were added to the OHM after the research was conducted, based on feedback from leaders participating in the Abundance Leadership Immersion Program.

Most readers of this book probably have an employee satisfaction or workplace culture survey that is done regularly. I recommend that those types of surveys be done every two years. Once a year is too frequent to allow for changes to go into place as a result of the feedback and, more important, for people to recognize that change has happened. There is a delay between changing a behavior, perceiving that the behavior is changed, and believing that the behavior is changed. I think three years is too long to wait for feedback about the organization's health because too many bad habits can become entrenched.

I also recommend that leaders get 360-degree feedback every two years, not once a year or every three years for the same reasons as just noted. I do not recommend 360-degree feedback for leaders of very small organizations such as OPG. It is too hard to ensure anonymity of the feedback providers. If you are working in or leading a small organization, you have to find other ways to get feedback, none of which provides the same opportunities of in-depth and detailed feedback that a good 360 instrument does.

Chapters 5 and 6 provide some sample big initiatives (macrolevers) and small steps (microlevers) to take to create a positive, creative, and abundant organization. As one Abundance Leadership Immersion Program alumni said, "The size of my organization is large, and it will take time and monumental effort to change the attitudes and effectiveness across the system." The ideas provided in the next two chapters can help.

CHAPTER 5

Macrolevers

You never change things by fighting the existing reality. To change something, build a new model that makes the existing model obsolete.

—Richard Buckminster (Bucky) Fuller

In this chapter, we'll explore the big changes you can make for a healthier organization: macrolevers. I will share four examples of these broader and deeper changes you can consider making to your organization. These changes are focused on increasing employee well-being and productivity simultaneously, and rethinking our historical conceptions of work, organizations, and power. Macrolevers take longer to implement and require more thoughtful planning and engagement with staff members and other leaders than microlevers, which we'll explore in Chapter 6.

We will look at four macrolevers: charrettes, the four-day workweek, workspace design, and circadian rhythm.

"... concentrated effort together with outstanding results ..."

—*Source unknown*

CHARRETTES

One way to shift the annual schedule while promoting innovation is by introducing a charrette, an intense period of design or planning, which is a common practice in the field of architecture and has recently been adopted across many industries. OPG undertook charrettes as an

This section is adapted from an article entitled "What's an Organizational Charrette, and How Can It Enhance Your Business?" that I cowrote with Robert Roche and Gretchen Wright for *HR Advisor* (2019).

experiment in 2017 and 2018 in order to test its impact on team creativity, productivity, and staff member engagement. We now hold a charrette every year.

What Is a Charrette?

Historically, a charrette is a process during which architects undergo an intensive working session to solve an architectural design problem and meet a deadline. According to *Wikipedia*, the term means "cart" or "chariot" in French and arose in the 19th century at the École des Beaux-Arts in Paris. There, it was not unusual for teams of student architects to work right up until a deadline at the end of a term, when a charrette (cart) would be wheeled among them to collect up their scale models and other work for review. Students would then continue to work furiously to apply the finishing touches on the way to the review. This came to be referred to as working *en charrette*, "in the cart."

Charrettes have a reputation of being intense, similar to pulling an all-nighter to complete a research paper or school project. In an article from the *Harvard Design Magazine*, author Daniel Willis (2010) writes that today, the term *charrette* is more commonly used to describe interactive brainstorming sessions among architects, as opposed to the grueling, deadline-driven, traditional charrette.

Nevertheless, the objective of the activity remains the same—solve a problem or create something innovative within a set period of time.

A Charrette at OPG

At OPG, a charrette is a predetermined period during which all employees stop regular operations for a specific length of time to dedicate themselves to creating or implementing one innovation for the company. (See Figure 5.1.) Employees can work on their innovation solo or in teams of any size. Project ideas are submitted a few weeks in advance to partners for approval. All employees present their project results at the end of the charrette.

Dedicating protected time and energy to a singular project produces benefits at both the individual and organizational levels. Individuals experience higher levels of creativity and engagement in the short term and increased job satisfaction in the long term.

Charrette Meeting and preparation process

6 months prior:

- Staff Meeting item—Introduction to the Charrette process and past research
- Schedule Charrette on all calendars
- Schedule preparation and follow up meetings

1 months prior:

- 1.5 hour all-staff meeting—Info session on Charrette, Q&A, and idea brainstorming session
- 1 hour all-staff meeting—Charrette project proposals
- Individual meetings with partners for feedback on projects
- Create feedback handouts and office schedule

1 week following:

- 2-hour all-staff meeting—Project presentations (if not completed end of week)
- Compile follow up and feedback documentation

FIGURE 5.1   Charrette prep instructions.

SOURCE: OPG.

At the organizational level, the process has produced completed projects that advance the whole organization (books to be published, strategy work, infrastructure solutions). In the long run, the process has increased the pace of business development.

It takes a bit of lift and logistics to conduct a charrette, especially the first one or two. Scheduling a full week without client work at a busy consulting firm means looking ahead six months. As scheduling gets underway, staff members are encouraged to start thinking about what they might want to accomplish during their charrette project. All staff members were required to generate a few ideas and to submit those ideas to the OPG leadership team. There are two criteria used to evaluate project ideas: the idea has to be mission-centric and financially viable.

To protect each staff member's time during charrette week, while acknowledging that client work at a consulting firm is necessary and ongoing, people check emails and respond to urgent client-related work before 8:30 a.m. and after 4:30 p.m. Charrette work takes place from 8:30 a.m. to 4:30 p.m., Monday through Thursday (we are on a four-day workweek). All OPG staff members post an out-of-office reply in their emails to alert clients of the charrette. These replies also include information on charrettes so clients can explore the concept on their own.

Approximately one month before the charrette, staff members share their planned projects at a staff meeting. Projects have ranged from writing a book about an organizational development topic to developing a new strategic marketing plan for OPG. The ideas are always diverse, and each project has differing needs. For example, an individual writer might prefer to work outside of the office, whereas a group project can need dedicated group work space within the office.

Questions arise about collaboration and whether there is time for feedback from one another during the week—especially from those not working on the same charrette project. At mid-week an all-staff lunch is held to check in on progress and help people problem-solve. Each person must plan how they will use their time throughout the charrette week, on a daily (and sometimes hourly) basis, to ensure that needs are met, everyone's time is respected, and work is supported.

At the end of the week prior to the charrettes, the staff members meet once more to go over logistics (email protocol, hours, who is working where, food, etc.), discuss expectations, and address any outstanding questions. In the first runs, each staff member was given a feedback data collection packet, which included a pre-charrette questionnaire that asked participants how they chose their project and about their charrette preparations:

- ➤ Cleared my calendar. Booked space to work.
- ➤ Did research on trends.
- ➤ (During the second year) Didn't do as much as last year.
- ➤ Conducted 5–7 hours of market research.

One piece of feedback from the second year of the charette from staff members was the need for OPG to be clearer about the scope of an OPG project and also the standard for the final presentation.

At the end of the charrettes, OPG staff members present their work and share their experiences doing the charrette (see Figure 5.2).

What did you get done?

- Two books, an
  onboarding process, and
  a kitchen cabinet
- Article
- Zoho Client "Brain Dump"

FIGURE 5.2   Results from an OPG charrette.
SOURCE: OPG.

This brings closure to the process and generates a list of next steps for moving unfinished projects forward. Some of the projects have had sustained results for OPG; some never got traction. That is to be expected and is part of innovating.

Organizations are always looking for ways to bolster innovation, keep staff members engaged, and maximize productivity. Charrettes are one powerful way to do so.

"The charrette was long, tiring, but good. The team feels great!"

FOUR-DAY WORKWEEK

Most of the companies participating in a four-day work-week pilot program in Britain said they had seen no loss of productivity during the experiment, and in some cases had seen a significant improvement . . .

—JENNY GROSS

OPG had been considering a four-day workweek for a couple of years before COVID hit. We had trouble imagining how we could serve our clients and complete all the tasks that were on everyone's plate within a four-day workweek. COVID was the catalyst for us to take that leap.

In the early days of COVID we were unsure about the financial impact on OPG, we cut all staff members' time to 60%. We noticed that we were still able to accomplish a great deal in three days a week. As we grew more confident about OPG's ability to weather the economic impact of COVID, we brought the staff members back up to 80% time, four days a week. Since then we have kept the four-day workweek, paying people 90% of their full-time equivalent salary.

As Leah Hancock, lead associate at OPG, wrote in a recent article,

> *It is not easy to untether ourselves from the only reality we know. And yet, if there was ever a time for a paradigm shift, this is it. For leaders of organizations and teams, the shift to a four-day workweek requires reimagining standard operating procedures, increasing innovation, and, perhaps most importantly, trusting in employees.*
>
> *Four-day workweek pilots are emerging across the globe, with some companies now shifting from the pilot phase to implementing the policy permanently. Microsoft Japan, Unilever, and Kickstarter represent just a few of a growing number of organizations exploring the four-day workweek.*
>
> *Proponents cite many benefits, including reduced burnout, improved physical and mental health, increased gender equity, and positive environmental impacts. It is easy to imagine what we might do with an additional day—spend time with family and friends, pursue a hobby, enroll in classes, become politically engaged, sleep. Many in favor of the four-day workweek envision a more fulfilled (and rested) community.*
>
> *Pilot findings show increased productivity as well. Microsoft Japan saw a 40% increase in productivity (measured in sales per employee) in their 2019 pilot, and New Zealand–based Perpetual Guardian, a trust management company, reported gains of 20%. Among companies that have adopted a four-day week, nearly two-thirds report increased productivity.*
>
> *Some leaders will see the research and be convinced that a pilot in their organization is worthwhile. Others will resist the idea. Leaders should get curious about any resistance that arises. What theories or beliefs are at the root of their concerns? Many leaders were taught that facetime with employees is the only way to ensure accountability, productivity, and teamwork. Less facetime, which is inherent to the four-day workweek model (and*

work-from-home arrangements), can feel to some like a loss of control. The leaders we need today lean into this discomfort and make decisions that will propel their organizations to be the best for their employees, their clients, their communities, and the world.

While each organization will need to find what works for them, doing so can be a productive exercise. Let employees work out the details rather than trying to "solve" the four-day work-week challenge from the top down. Perpetual Guardian asked employees to propose their own productivity measures, including how they and their teams would increase productivity, and to coordinate time off. Awin, a Berlin-based tech firm, saw 80 employees volunteer for task forces to ensure that their switch to a four-day workweek went smoothly. Those who are closest to the work and potential challenges are often closest to the solutions. The website www.4dayweek.com also offers many resources to help companies design a four-day workweek pilot. (Hancock 2021)

Abundance leaders are open to trying new and creative ways of working, such as the four-day workweek. These experiments convey trust in staff members, and they convey a curious and open mindset on the part of the leader, a strong trait in Abundance leaders. Trying new ways of working helps staff members feel safe breaking out of old paradigms in other ways, and helps foster a culture of innovation.

WORKSPACE DESIGN

Why would you design something if it didn't improve the human condition?

—Niels Diffrient

I grew up in a family of architects and was surrounded by art and design conversations from a young age. I remember clearly going into my father's architecture offices and looking at the blueprints, models, and drawings. I remember hearing my father and step-mother (partners in their firm) talking with colleagues about how one thinks about space and design and their impact on human beings. My father once quoted an architect who said that a person does not live only in the space at eye level. Because our eyes can see to every corner of a room, we experience and live in the entire space.

As a result of my upbringing, I have paid special attention to creating both home and workspaces that are warm, welcoming, light-filled, and contribute to productivity. I think cubicles are like small prisons. They are demeaning and diminishing and make it very clear what the hierarchy is in an organization. I know that as a leader, you want to do better than cubicles. I encourage you to get creative, think out of the box, literally. And reach out for design help if you need it. Designers are partners in creating extraordinary cultures.

Engage your staff members and design professionals in rethinking the design of your offices. As one enters into a space, initial impressions are made about what the organization values, what it is like to work there, how they treat employees, how customers are treated, and more.

FIGURE 5.3   OPG's main conference room—the Aquarium.
SOURCE: OPG/Tony Panos.

The human mind is so quick, agile, and robust that it reads all sorts of data quickly and makes assumptions and decisions about its environment.

> *Spaces can be designed to favor exploration or engagement or energy to achieve certain outcomes. For example, if a call center wants improved productivity, the space should favor engagement—getting the team to interact more. Higher engagement is typically accomplished not with open social space but with tight, walled-off workstations and adjacent spaces for small-group collaboration and interaction. The team's break area becomes a crucial collision space. At one call center, the company expanded the break room and gave reps more time to hang out there with colleagues. Paradoxically, productivity shot up after the change. Away from their phones, the reps could circulate knowledge within the group. (Waber, Magnolfi, and Lindsay 2014)*

Staff members, and you, need great spaces in which to thrive, where a meeting, retreat, or any gathering produces the alchemy of great ideas about organizations, and where a vision for a better world comes to life. (See Figures 5.3, 5.4, and 5.5.)

MANAGING BY CIRCADIAN RHYTHM

Always be a first-rate version of yourself and not a second-rate version of someone else.

—JUDY GARLAND

Finding an opportunity to improve in a difficult and challenging situation is what Abundance Leadership is all about. If there is one thing that we have learned in the last few months of the COVID-19 crisis, it is that the ability to be flexible, creative, and adaptable may be the strongest currency an organization can possess. Those organizations that have the ability to operate "from home" are quickly learning that the 9 a.m. to 5 p.m. paradigm we lived under for so many decades may be unnecessary and even detrimental to productivity.

FIGURE 5.4   Clients in OPG's Aquarium conference room.

SOURCE: Organizational Performance Group.

Are we really 100% productive from mid-morning to early evening, five days a week? For most, if not all, the answer is a definite no. A new organizational paradigm is pulling us away from the 9–5, and the decision remains with leaders on whether to explore or ignore our own circadian rhythms and modify the outdated ideas about work schedules.

After decades of leading people and organizations, I remain challenged in creating work environments that allow staff members to work in ways that honor their circadian rhythms and thus, one assumes, increase their productivity and health. At OPG, for example, one of our

FIGURE 5.5   OPG's Aquarium conference room with moveable furniture for all types of group work.

SOURCE: OPG/Tony Panos.

staff members is most effective in the afternoon and would prefer to begin working at noon and working into the evening. Another staff member needs to work from home on Fridays so she can tie up all her loose ends before the weekend. (This research was done before OPG had a four-day workweek.) And yet another staff member likes to start their day at 7 a.m. and leave at 3 p.m. How do we construct an organization that has room for these energy patterns and feels productive, trusting, and delivers on its promises to clients?

To begin to get some insights, I asked the staff members at OPG if they would be willing to serve as an initial lab for exploring this persistent management dilemma. OPG's staff members are accustomed to participating in lab experiments. We are clear in our recruitment materials and our mission statement that we use OPG to test management, leadership, and organizational techniques. We've tried self-managed time off and charrettes, among other programs and policies.

The OPG staff members agreed to the experiment, so I gave them forms to fill out asking them to share their energy levels at different points in a day, in a week, and each month of the year. I used the following scale:

1. Need time off
2. Need to slow down
3. On the fence
4. Somewhat productive time
5. Prime work time

The resulting data are shown in Figure 5.6.

For daily energy flow, the data show that people have varying waves of energy during the day. Some rise, stay up, and then fall at the end of the day. Three people get an additional spike of energy late in the day. Ten in the morning seems to be a high point in energy for everyone; at OPG, our staff meetings usually start at this time. And, no one has much energy before 5 a.m. (Figure 5.7).

The weekly energy flow is more consistent across the group of eight, with everyone having a dip on Friday. Two people get an upward spike on the weekend. The universal dip on Friday raised the question of a

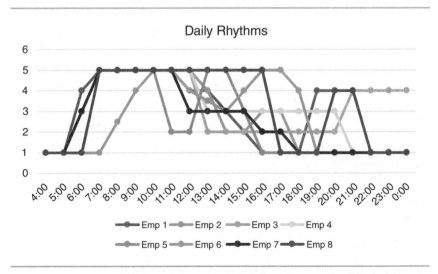

FIGURE 5.6 OPG staff member circadian rhythm by time of day.

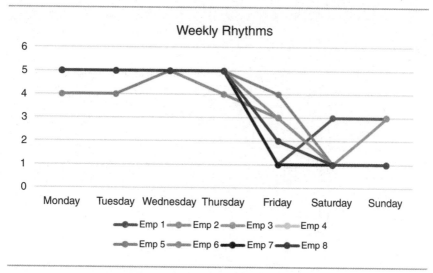

FIGURE 5.7   Circadian rhythm by day of the week.

four-day workweek, with longer days (which might run counter to the daily energy flow) or with weekend work.

The annual energy flow shows a slight dip in March and April and a deeper decline in energy in August and December. The data raised the question of whether the August and December dips are culturally conditioned or a true energy dip at that time of year (Figure 5.8).

Possible Guidelines for Creating a Circadian-Friendly Work Environment

I spent time thinking about guidelines for a circadian-friendly work environment:

➤ Client needs must be met.
➤ Everyone must be in the office at times that their job function demands.
➤ Everyone works at least 40 hours.
➤ Everyone must be in on Monday.
➤ Everyone must be in the office at least 24 hours/week.
➤ Working from home outside of the 40 hours is up to individual.
➤ Everyone must be at staff meetings.
➤ Weekly schedule must be posted in public place.

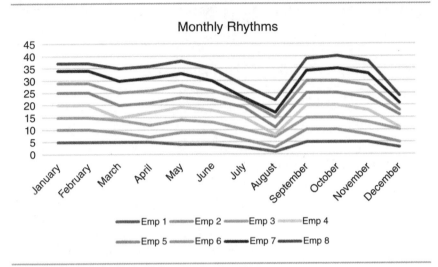

FIGURE 5.8 Circadian rhythm by month.

> Each person's schedule can change week to week, month to month, depending on their needs.
> Earliest start is 6 a.m.
> Latest end at the office is 7 p.m.
> Tele-meetings with colleagues are fine.

This list seemed too long and counter to a culture of self-management. In conversation with OPG's chief operating officer, Tammy Astarita, we developed a set of five "min specs" (minimum specifications; see Liberating Structures website [www.liberatingstructures.org] for more on min specs) that were used for the experiment:

> Be easily locatable.
> Give and get adequate face time.
> Get your work done on time and to OPG's standards.
> Do what YOU need to do; "you do you."
> No meetings on Fridays.

Another habit we started as part of this experiment was to share our monthly deliverables at the beginning of each month, and then provide an update at the end of the month.

Key Insights from the Data from Discussions with Staff Members

During our experiment, each person in the office went through their upcoming schedule and decided when they would be working, when they would be off, and when they would be in the office or at home. As our firm was growing quickly, we experienced an above-average amount of work during this period, making for an ideal experimental environment. Throughout the period, every employee took lab notes on what was working and what was a challenge, using the min specs as a reference to comment on.

At a meeting with the staff members to debrief the first month of the experiment, many comments were shared. Here's a sample:

> Short lab notes; not a lot of notes taken
> How do we know or trust that someone can manage this?
> How much should people be alone in their first three to six months at OPG?
> Forgot we were doing it
> Every role needs to ensure coverage.
> Calendars must be up-to-date.
> Office must be occupied for phones and visitors?
> Speaks to OPG's investment in the team.
> Leadership needs to model it.
> Keep "no meeting Fridays."
> Revisit four-day workweek.
> Need to be flexible about your schedule for others.

Next, the staff members shared some pros and cons about using this model. The pros included the following:

> No meetings on Fridays
> Five min specs
> Didn't feel like people were unavailable or didn't follow specs
> Felt rested and relaxed
> Didn't feel judged for coming and going
> Felt greater trust; reciprocal
> Allowed time for deeper interactions between individuals
> Increased commitment

The cons included the following:

➤ Always should have someone at the front desk and running phones
➤ Guilt (when leaving) because of anticipated judgment

Last, the staff members shared the questions that came up during the discussion:

➤ Should OPG run this as a lab test for one quarter in 2019?
➤ What about when a new person joins OPG?
  ○ Does the 24-hour/week not apply to them for some period of time?
  ○ Does it mean everyone must "up" their in-office time for x amount of time as the new person is onboarding?
➤ Will the weekly schedule be posted in a public place electronically?

Results

Since the experiment, OPG has defaulted to a modified circadian rhythm work schedule without much formality. Each staff member has defined their preferred daily and weekly schedule within a wide framework. For example, the OPG day runs from 7 a.m. to 6 p.m. Staff members build their daily schedule inside that broader schedule. Staff members continue to use and abide by the five guiding principles, previously described as the min specs:

➤ Be easily locatable.
➤ Give and get adequate face time.
➤ Get your work done on time and to OPG's standards.
➤ Do what YOU need to do; "you do you."
➤ No meetings on Fridays. (This is no longer relevant at OPG because we have a four-day workweek, and we do "all-in" Mondays. All staff members are in-person in the office on Mondays; from Tuesday to Thursday, staff self-manage whether they are working from home or the office.)

I think the staff members would agree that a modified circadian rhythm system works well but only if there is a culture of trust, high-performing people, and strong self-management skills. As a leader, I would not advocate for a full free-form circadian rhythm schedule in our industry. There are just too many essential points of connection that would fray. And, frankly, we do not have strong enough productivity measures for me to feel confident that all staff members are meeting most of their targets on time, a condition I think must be met before someone is self-scheduling. That seems like a bit of a catch-22: if a circadian-based schedule makes you more productive, then why not start there so staff members can meet their targets?

It may take decades more to find our new rhythm as a workforce. The simple reality is that there may be more pandemics, more curveballs that challenge what is normal about working in an office from 9 a.m. to 5 p.m., Monday through Friday. As leaders we must become dedicated to meeting the demands of our industry and the needs of our workforce that make them the most productive. As an Abundance leader, it is up to you to be creative and flexible because your team will need those traits more than ever.

CHAPTER **6**

Microlevers: Small Tools for Big Change

The journey of a thousand miles begins with one step.

—LAO TZE

Do small things with great love.

—MOTHER THERESA

The ultimate point of being an Abundance leader is to have a healthy organization that is productive, profitable, and has a positive impact on the world. Getting your organization to good health takes attention and effort. And, vice versa: healthy organizations are a beneficial result of Abundance Leadership. Getting your organization to better health does not have to be only about major change initiatives. Small acts can create big waves of positive culture.

In this chapter, I'll share seven of these microlevers that we use at OPG:

➤ The gong
➤ The annual donation—collective competition for the greater good
➤ Public agenda—speak up and be heard
➤ Community wall
➤ Snow globes and collective memory
➤ Facilitation rotation
➤ Dream list

Dynamic, healthy, and appropriate organizational cultures and climates lift morale, which in turn increases effectiveness, in turn creating an even healthier culture and climate. Difficult and dysfunctional cultures and climates work in the opposite direction, dragging down results and diminishing morale.

Leaders often think of culture change and improvement as a huge undertaking requiring significant organizational lift and involving extensive plans, hundreds of meetings, and big expenditures. Well, it does help to have a vision, a strategy, and a set of goals that define the desired culture, but culture change is also enacted at the micro level in small acts, minor adjustments, and microlevers.

OPG helps our clients get going with culture change by encouraging them to implement microlevers immediately; start doing things and acting differently, and the culture will follow. First, we ask Abundance leaders to reflect deeply on their personal values and the changes they want to see in the world, not just in their organization. Then they can begin to manifest those values and vision inside their organization with small acts and changes—what we call *microlevers*.

What is a microlever? A microlever is a practical, nitty-gritty tactic implemented visibly and consistently. They have impact in and of themselves, but they also serve as a signal to the organization. Microlevers are small acts with big signaling impact—small steps or actions that tell people "things are different here." Or "things are getting better." Or "you matter."

OPG works with our clients to figure out the right microlevers for their organizations, and we help them take the first steps now to change their organization's culture. For more on microlevers, check out our series of short podcasts (about five minutes each) at "OPG Inspire Podcast."

THE GONG

OPG has a "good news gong" in the middle of our open atrium space (see Figure 6.1). The gong is rung whenever a contract is landed, when the firm achieves a major goal, when a staff member has good personal news to share, or when any other good news, worthy of sharing, happens. When the gong is rung, everyone comes out of their office to the public space to hear the news.

FIGURE 6.1   OPG's good news gong.

SOURCE: OPG/Tony Panos.

THE ANNUAL DONATION: COLLECTIVE COMPETITION
FOR THE GREATER GOOD

At OPG we have a tradition that engages our staff members in improving the world, while engaging our clients and extended community. Every year in December we ask the staff members to nominate a nonprofit of their choice to be part of a list of nonprofits that might receive a donation from OPG. The combined list of nonprofits is turned into a survey that is sent out to our entire database.

Everyone in the database is welcome to vote for the nonprofit of their choice to receive OPG's annual donation. The survey is usually sent out in January after the holidays so it does not get lost in the holiday madness. Once we know which nonprofit is receiving our annual donation, we send the donation with a letter explaining how they were chosen. Recent recipients of the donation include Equal Justice Initiative and Green Village Initiative. Staff members are always hopeful that their nonprofit "won" the donation. We exclude OPG clients from possible donation recipients to avoid any appearance of pandering.

PUBLIC AGENDA: SPEAK UP AND GET HEARD

Here's another example of a microlever: put up a blank flipchart in your organization's common area. Write "topics for next staff meeting" at the top. Add below that, "Please put your name next to anything you list so you can help lead the discussion." Put a magic marker nearby. See what happens. Add to it. Now use the list as items on the next staff meeting agenda. You should see higher engagement of staff members and more transparency.

COMMUNITY WALL: LIFE OUTSIDE OF WORK

OPG has a space in one of our hallways where people can post pictures of their loved ones and activities from outside of work (see Figure 6.2). The

FIGURE 6.2   The OPG "who are you outside of work" gallery.
SOURCE: OPG/Tony Panos.

gallery increases people's sense of each other's full lives, and it reminds us that there is more to life than work. Yes, work can be a beautiful end in and of itself when it has a positive impact on the world and is purpose driven. Yet, work is also there to serve as a way of supporting the rest of our life.

SNOW GLOBES AND COLLECTIVE MEMORY

My stepmother had the habit of collecting snow globes. When I started the Learning Center at Yale, I brought that habit into the department. I asked people to buy snow globes whenever they traveled, and we put them on a shelf in a public space. This habit came over to OPG as well and was expanded.

At OPG, we not only collect snow globes from our personal travels but also from our work travels, and we have added to the collection a variety of memorabilia from our consulting engagements (see Figure 6.3).

FIGURE 6.3 **The OPG "share your travels" shelves.**

SOURCE: OPG/Tony Panos.

We keep table tents, signage, and other items irrespective of our work. Stuffed animals from a visit to the Disney campus in Burbank. A leg lamp from a visit to the house where the "The Christmas Story" was filmed in Cleveland.

FACILITATION ROTATION

At OPG we have many formats for staff gatherings. For three of those in particular, we rotate facilitation. We have half-hour biweekly check-ins; a monthly extended full staff meeting that runs two hours; and, an annual two-day retreat. For all three of these meetings, we rotate the facilitator role through all staff members, no matter what their role is at OPG. The front desk staff, the consulting staff, the administrative staff, and all OPGers take turns designing the agendas and facilitating the meetings. For the annual two-day retreat, because it is a significant design and facilitation lift, there are usually two OPG staff members working together.

This habit of rotating facilitation achieves many ends that benefit the individual staff members and OPG. The staff members learn how to lead a meeting, develop their public presence, and develop other subtle skills that will help them in their career, whether that career is at OPG or somewhere else. For OPG, we all get the benefit of fresh ideas and more effective colleagues.

DREAM LIST: IMAGINING OUR IDEAL WORLD

Another microlever we use at OPG is the annual dream list. We sometimes do this at the annual retreat, or the end-of-year celebration, or at an end-of-year meeting. It's very simple. As a group, we generate a list of all the things we wish we had at OPG. Current items on the dream list are a helicopter, a coffee machine that says I love you, and a dishwasher. Some items stay on the dream list forever, and some can be realized very quickly by the leadership team making quick decisions to change aspects of OPG or purchasing certain items.

Small acts. Big returns. Microlevers.

Tips and Activities for Microlevers

> ➤ Paint a wall with whiteboard paint so people can cocreate more easily.
> ➤ Create a wall on which people can hang or post pictures of people and things outside work that matter to them (refer to Figure 6.3).
> ➤ Post your meeting norms in every room.
> ➤ Flatten your hierarchy and distance between staff members by "chopping wood and carrying water." In modern terms, as the leader, this means washing the dishes, cleaning off the table, and otherwise stopping to help with the mundane tasks of organizational life.
> ➤ Try out innovative management practices.
> ➤ Have everyone in the office wear nametags when a new person is coming on board.
> ➤ Pay attention to your physical space. What does the design of it signal about the organization's values?

SECTION III

The How-to Manual

You'll never plow a field by turning it over in your mind.

—IRISH PROVERB

This section does a deep dive into the behaviors and competencies that Abundance leaders exhibit, and it includes tips and techniques for you to use to enact those behaviors and competencies.

"The value of an idea lies in the using of it."

—Thomas Edison

The Abundance Leadership model tends to make intuitive sense to leaders and managers who read about it. However, a model is only useful if it works in real life. The prior sections of the book include broad statements about behaviors and competencies and some macro- and micro-lever suggestions. In this section, I want to give you concrete actions and techniques you can try to make your Abundance Leadership mental model come to life.

The tips and techniques in this section are not the be-all-end-all of possible things you can do to enact Abundance Leadership, nor do they represent OPG's complete portfolio of advice we give leaders. These tips and techniques are shared to stimulate your thinking. If you don't find what you need, reach out to us at OPG, do some web searching, reach out to your mentors, or ask your staff members for ideas.

As a reminder and as I shared in Chapter 3, Table S3.1 here shows the relationship among meta-competencies, competencies, and behaviors. We'll be doing a deep dive into the behaviors in this section of the book.

TABLE S3.1   The Abundance Leadership Competencies

Meta-Competency	Competency	Abundance Behavior
Visioning	Visioning	Has a compelling vision that they are able to communicate and on which they build their organization
		Builds on the past but is not constrained by it
		Thinks in the long term and the big picture
		Exudes and conveys energy and hope for good outcomes
		Focuses on the bottom line—is financially savvy
	Creativity	Seeks creative and alternative ways of solving problems
		Has high technical expertise
		Has high cognitive intelligence
Visibility	Visibility	Manages by walking around; is visible to staff members
		Does not hide in their office; maximizes contact with others
Self-Awareness	Reflection and affect	Seeks out the opinion and energy of others when appropriate
		Is rarely ruffled and keeps an even tone and affect in most situations
		Manages their time well

Meta-Competency	Competency	Abundance Behavior
	Interpersonal adeptness	Demonstrates empathy and compassion for others
		Gives their attention and kindness without effort
		Addresses conflict
	Morality	Has a strong moral compass that is evident in their language and actions
		Is trustworthy
	Ego control	Is humble
		Is not egocentric; does not have a "me, me" attitude
Managing Well	Team building	Looks for opportunities to build teams
		Understands and articulates the role others play in the success of the team
		Delegates
		Guides and challenges employees so that they develop
	Communication	Proactively shares as much information as possible
		Seeks out feedback and receives it with openness; willingly learns from mistakes
	Protection	Protects staff members from abusive conditions
		Seeks out resources and is able to gain resources for their staff members
		Maintains healthy organizational and psychological boundaries for themselves and their team[*]
	Decision-making	Is decisive
		Does not make inappropriately dictatorial decisions

[*]This behavior is not part of the original research and has been added as the model has been applied.

CHAPTER 7

Visioning

The visionary starts with a clean sheet of paper and
re-imagines the world.

—MALCOLM GLADWELL

Visionary people face the same problems everyone else
faces; but rather than get paralyzed by their problems,
visionaries immediately commit themselves to finding
a solution.

—BILL HYBELS

Meta-Competency	Competency	Abundance Behavior
Visioning	Visioning	Has a compelling vision that they are able to communicate and on which they build their organization
		Builds on the past but is not constrained by it
		Thinks in the long term and the big picture
		Exudes and conveys energy and hope for good outcomes
		Focuses on the bottom line—is financially savvy
	Creativity	Seeks creative and alternative ways of solving problems
		Has high technical expertise
		Has high cognitive intelligence

VISIONING

As discussed in Chapter 3, the competency of visioning is fundamental to a leader's ability to keep their organization's ecosystem healthy. There are five abundance behaviors related to this competency. Let's look at each one and ways to practice those behaviors.

Behavior: Has a Compelling Vision That They Are Able to Communicate and on Which They Build Their Organization

We looked at this from a meta-competency perspective in Chapter 3. Let's do a deeper dive here into visioning competencies and behaviors.

What is your vision for your organization? Can you easily articulate it, and do you share it regularly in a variety of settings? It is your vision, ideally shared by your staff members, that will propel your organization to success, attract staff and board members, guide decisions and choices, and inspire people to weather any storms.

Here are some examples of company vision statements:

➤ Southwest Airlines: "To become the world's most loved, most flown and most profitable airline."
➤ Ben & Jerry's: "Making the best ice cream in the nicest possible way."
➤ LinkedIn: "Create economic opportunity for every member of the global workforce."
➤ Habitat for Humanity: "A world where everyone has a decent place to live."
➤ Prezi: "To reinvent how people share knowledge, tell stories, and inspire their audiences to act."

As discussed in Chapter 3, I encourage you to articulate your personal vision for a better world and lead from there. Create a vision that will guide you in all your decisions, one that is an inspiration for others, a vision on which your company can coalesce and one that your staff members, at the end of their days, will say was worth spending their lives on.

Bolman and Deal (1995) lay out a prescription for bringing spirit and élan into the workplace. "Leaders with soul bring spirit to organizations" (p. 10). They write about reconnecting to a whole part of ourselves, transcendent of science and materialism. According to Bolman and

Deal, leaders should help employees transcend fear, engage in dialogue, and have an increased sense of community. You can do this through creating a vision for your organization and for yourself.

Here are three concepts to help you start or nuance your vision. The first is planning for the seventh generation. As mentioned previously Chief Lyons said, "What about the seventh generation? Where are you taking them? What will they have?" Consider sublimating short-term and individual gains for the longer-term health of the planet and community. Maybe there is a little less profit this quarter because you have changed your product's packaging to an eco-friendly solution. The longer-term gain for humanity is worth it.

The second concept is to operate from a wide-open heart, from an abundance mentality. Assume the best. Assume it will be okay. I do not think it is easy to stay open-hearted. It is not irrational to feel angry, tired, defensive, or other similar emotions. Being open-hearted is the practice of working through those emotions to the other side where you have learned from them and can better see them arising and put them to better use. I don't think it's about getting rid of these strong negative emotions. It's about using them appropriately.

The last concept is that beauty matters. Beautiful aesthetics are motivators in their own right and create connection. Remember what it is like to see a beautiful piece of art or to enter into a gorgeous space. Nature also offers its own version of an astounding aesthetic; picture the Grand Canyon or Mt. Everest. In your work—in your spaces, materials, products, office surroundings—I encourage you to create beauty. It rarely costs any more than dullness.

Grounding your leadership in your own personal vision for your life and your work can increase your sense of direction and purpose and can be a role model for staff members. Most people do not have a personal vision statement. A personal vision enables you to align both your personal and professional visions, gives you a clearly defined road map for your own personal success ("if you fail to plan, you are planning to fail"), and gives you inspiration to always be looking toward the future.

I suggest to my coaching clients that they start by imagining themselves at 85 years old. They are sitting on a porch looking out over a beautiful vista. They might or might not have a loved one with them. The two of them are reminiscing about their life and what they have accomplished. They play back the years of work, family, travels, loved ones, adventures,

> **Sample personal vision statement**
>
> "Further develop and use my passion for listening and facilitating to help those who want to achieve their best. Become an accessible resource to tap into to help those who want to explore and become their very best in leading and interpersonal relationships."

FIGURE 7.1 Sample personal vision statement.

SOURCE: OPG.

risks, failures, disappointments, and all the parts of a life that make it full and rich and meaningful. I ask them to notice what this future vision implies for their current reality. What does this vision for a full life suggest that they need to do now? Or that they have already accomplished?

I then suggest that they imagine themselves at 65. They are at a retirement party with people who truly care about them in a deep way. They are getting up to give a speech to the gathered friends and colleagues. What would they say to this group about their work life? About how work and home life intersected? About their impact on the world? Again, I ask them to reflect on what this vision for 65 implies about changes they need to make now, things they have already accomplished, or any other thoughts they have about a personal vision (see Figure 7.1).

Here are some questions to help you create a personal vision:

- ➤ What is your "why?" Can you define yourself in three words?
- ➤ In what areas of your business do you love working? What areas energize you?
- ➤ Given the opportunity, what job functions would you delegate?
- ➤ Outside of money, what intangible benefits do you require from your work?
- ➤ What, if any, are your spiritual beliefs that bring you contentment?

- What do you like doing for me-time? What are your hobbies or interests?
- What do you want to achieve in the future that would bring personal satisfaction?
- How much family time do you want, and what will you do with it?

Behaviors: (1) Builds on the Past but Is Not Constrained by It and (2) Thinks in the Long Term and the Big Picture

When we take over a position as a leader, it is advisable to first seek to understand what the organization's history is about and what it has been through recently. We have been hired often to repair problems in the organization and to take it to the next level. It is tempting to blame people from the organization's past or past decisions. I have done this myself, too frequently. However, this does not reflect well on the new leader. Ideally, we keep our comments respectful of the past and repair past issues by creating new directions. Strategic planning is one way to bring the past respectfully into the future.

Strategic planning is essential to help your entire organization move in the same direction, toward a shared vision, and to build on the past while not being constrained by it. Most organizations now have strategic plans. I do want to say a few words about strategic planning here because visions are usually part of a strategic plan. I think you can have a leadership vision, your own particular vision, for your organization and for how you lead. It is also important to have a shared cocreated vision for your organization. That is where a strategic plan can be helpful.

OPG defines a successful strategic planning process as one that accomplishes the following:

- Produces a written plan that is appropriately ambitious and focused
- Generates energy and enthusiasm for the organization's future among leadership, staff members, volunteers, donors, community members, and other key constituents
- Develops relevant and applicable skills among all individuals involved, including in the areas of leadership, management, facilitation, and communication
- Creates stronger, more engaged organizational citizens and builds camaraderie among staff members and key constituents engaged in the process

Most strategic plans have the following elements: vision, mission, organizational values, success measures (see my article on "Radically Transformative Indicators" on OPG's website, www.orgpg.com, under the Resources section), goals, strategies, initiatives, and tactics. Strategic planning should generally be done every three to five years, and the planning process itself should enhance the organization's culture and further its mission.

You can create a strategic planning process that includes ways for the staff members and the community to process past events and use the insights gained to move forward together. When we were doing strategic planning for a large organization, in the exploratory phase of the project we realized that they had had five leaders in five years. One of those leaders had died in their office. Another one of the leaders had been asked to leave due to some problematic behavior. As a result of these leadership changes, the community had grief and anxiety. To kick off the strategic planning process, we worked with all of the staff and board members to process what had happened and develop insights that they could pull forward into their strategic plan.

Bringing your strategic plan to life and imbuing the entire organization with its direction takes effort. OPG helped create strategic plans for the Yale University Art Gallery, then under the direction of Jock Reynolds, the gallery director. One day, a few months after the plan was complete, I went over to the storage facility to meet Jock for a meeting. Of course, the security was very high for that facility, and there was a guard there who took my ID and contacted Jock to let him know that I was there. The guard asked me, "While you're waiting for Jock would you like to hear about the gallery's mission?" This was such a powerful indicator that the mission and strategic plan of the gallery were reaching all staff members. There are many ways to bring a strategic plan to life but I will save that for another book.

Another method to help you and your staff members see the long-term patterns and direction of your organization is to normalize events, problems, and other parts of organizational life. Instead of pathologizing or catastrophizing, try normalizing. What does that mean?

When we are raising children, we do not tell the two-year-old that they have a pathological problem because they are in diapers. We know they will outgrow diapers in the natural course of their development. Everything has a natural course of development—groups, teams, organizations, dogs, trees. When you know what "normal" is for any living thing or any type of project or organization, then you can normalize behavior, problems, and successes, and avoid pathologizing. Pathologizing, much like judging, makes a problem intractable and creates a personal or institutional sense of shame and ineffectiveness.

One way to stop yourself from pathologizing anyone is to avoid using a conjugation of the verb *to be*. When you say, "you are . . . ," you might be pathologizing. For example, "You are selfish," is much more damning than, "You are behaving in a selfish way." When you say, "Right now I notice you are doing . . . ," you are more likely to be normalizing. Practice completing the sentence, "This is normal because . . ."

Abundance leaders are able to normalize events, successes, and problems for their staff members. They use language such as, "We are in start-up mode so it's to be expected that our policies are not fully formed."

Do your best to meet people, and your organization, where they are developmentally, without shame or blame. Remember that people are doing the best they can with the information they have, so if there is a problem, ask what information they are working with, and if appropriate, try giving them more information as a first step.

Behavior: Exudes and Conveys Energy and Hope for Good Outcomes

I have already written quite a bit in this book about optimism, which is one of the foundations for this particular Abundance Leadership behavior—exuding energy and hope. Abundance leaders will acknowledge difficulties and hard times but will not wallow. They process difficult moments but move their staff members to think about the upside of the hard moment.

My mother says, "Hard times are gifts in strange wrappings." I think this embodies the positive, optimistic leader that most people want to work for. The ability to exude optimism, see opportunity in difficulty, and stay energized in the face of difficulty are wonderful attributes. Of course, these can be taken too far and be seen as pollyannaish and foolish. But in the main, these characteristics help people sustain their energy to move forward.

It is important, therefore, that you as a leader sustain your own health and well-being. In Chapter 9, I go into self-care briefly. This is a mandate I am sure you have heard before, and there is much written about it.

If you are dealing with a potentially scary outcome, practice hoping for the best and preparing for the worst. Imagine all possible outcomes in the situation, from the worst to the best. This is important. Imagine the worst-case scenario: What would you do in that situation? Be specific. Think about the details and steps required to survive and thrive in the worst-case scenario. Do this until your fear of the worst-case scenario decreases. When we are ready for the worst, we can be more present.

Behavior: Focuses on the Bottom Line—Is Financially Savvy

My training is in the field of organizational development. Sometimes I am asked to speak to people about my career and my educational trajectory in my field. I am a strong believer in the value of finance and accounting as a critical field of study for all leaders. Money is a form of energy. It is how we as human beings transfer our energy from one entity to another; it's how we measure the value of our time.

Because money is one of the key forms, if not *the* key form, of energy transfer that undergirds an organization, it is a critical element to understand. I cannot overemphasize the need to understand not just the fundamentals of accounting, finance, and budgeting but also the psychological impact of these areas on your staff members.

When asked by young people whether they should get a masters in organizational leadership or organizational development versus an MBA, I always suggest the MBA. It lays the foundational understanding of all elements of organizational life.

Tips and Activities for Visioning

- Vision repetition:
  1. Have a vision for your organization.
  2. Share the vision.
  3. Translate the vision into meaningful work.
  4. Repeat steps 1–3 over and over again.
- Create a strategic plan with your staff members.
- Normalize by using the sentence, "This is normal because . . ."
- Understand your organization's finances as deeply as possible.

CREATIVITY

Creativity is critical to good leadership, not only because it helps the company innovate in its revenue lines but also helps create a transformative culture. It is often hard for staff members to be creative without help and training. I believe this fear of innovation is the result of our culture in the United States, and in many countries, that reinforces or requires a narrow band of acceptable public behavior. Schools, religious organizations, families, and other organizations spend a great deal of time and resources working on keeping people "in line." Try getting in an elevator and facing the back of it for the ride. People will think you're crazy.

When I teach team building I do an exercise in which teams have to build a tower using large sticky notes and paper clips, a tower that will meet three criteria: height, aesthetics, and stability. The exact phrase I use is, "You must use paper clips and sticky notes." Of the participants 90% stick with the sticky notes and paper clips. Why? They assume they can *only* use sticky notes and paper clips. They also sit at the table diligently working on small designs, not using any other surfaces (i.e., walls).

The most creative groups are usually the graduate students in my seminars. I had one group of students stand their tallest member up on the table and then cover him with sticky notes. It is this kind of out-of-the-box thinking that is so helpful to organizations and to the planet. And yet many of our classrooms and other institutions focus on producing obedient people who do exactly as they are told. The historical forces, underlying societal drivers, and policies that create this type of classroom are the subject of thousands of books and discussions, and are of concern to educators around the world. You can find ways to help you and your staff members get out of mental straitjackets. One of the Abundance Leadership Program alumni told me, "With the restructure, we're finding new opportunities and efficiencies all the time. The program helped by opening our minds and giving us a 'hall pass' to think and act differently."

I had the privilege of having parents who sought out alternative education settings for me, beginning with Montessori in Rome as a small child, going on to some home schooling mixed in with public school, and then high school in an alternative forward-thinking school in San Francisco called the Urban School of San Francisco. These alternative learning settings, with teachers who encouraged questioning the rules, critical thinking, and creativity, have served me well my entire life.

I encourage you as a leader to look for ways to help your staff members see the boxes that they, you, or your organization are in and explore ways to break out of those boxes.

Behavior: Seeks Creative and Alternative Ways of Solving Problems

Creativity is helpful in many more ways than we often think. Even small creative solutions can yield positive results. Several years ago, OPG was working on a strategic plan for a large nonprofit. Possible revenue shortfalls were of primary concern, as they are for almost all nonprofits. The chief operating officer suggested a small, out-of-the-box idea—charge for parking. This sounds minor but the museum had always advertised free parking. The idea was implemented, and it added over $200K to the museum's bottom line. Complaints were minor and faded quickly.

A *Harvard Business Review* article about 3M's programs to encourage creativity and innovation provides a solid framework and ideas for programs you can add to your organization.

> [I]nnovators share common qualities, which we call the innovation mindset, a robust framework which can be applied at the micro (individual) as well as macro (organizational) levels: they see and act on opportunities, use "and" thinking to resolve tough dilemmas and break through compromises, and employ their resourcefulness to power through obstacles. Innovators maintain a laser focus on outcomes, avoid getting caught in the activity trap, and proactively "expand the pie" to make an impact. Regardless of where they start, innovators and innovative companies persist till they successfully change the game.
>
> Take, for example, 3M Corporation. 3M was awarded the US government's highest award for innovation, the National Medal of Technology.
>
> One critical balance at 3M is between present AND future concerns. Quarterly results are important but should not be the sole focus; staying relevant is also important but cannot come at the cost of current performance. 3M has several mechanisms to sustain this "and thinking." Employing the Thirty Percent Rule, 30% of each division's revenues must come from products introduced in the last four years. This is tracked rigorously, and employee bonuses are based on successful achievement of this goal. 3M also uses "and

thinking" in their three-tiered research structure. Each research area has a unique focus: Business Unit Laboratories focus on specific markets, with near-term products; Sector Laboratories, on applications with 3- to 10-year time horizons; and Corporate Laboratories, on basic research with a time horizon of as long as 20 years. Innovative companies create systems, structures, and work environments to encourage resourcefulness and initiative.

3M has a rich set of structures and systems to encourage resourcefulness:

> *Seed Capital: Inventors can request seed capital from their business unit managers; if their request is denied, they can seek funding from other business units. Inventors can also apply for corporate funding in the form of a Genesis Grant. (The Post-it was funded by a Genesis Grant.)*
> *New Venture Formation: Product inventors must recruit their own teams, reaping the benefit of 3M's many networking forums as they seek the right people for the job at hand. The recruits have a chance to evaluate the inventor's track record before signing up. However, if the product fails, everyone is guaranteed their previous jobs.*
> *Dual-career ladder: Scientists can continue to move up the ladder without becoming managers. They have the same prestige, compensation, and perks as corporate management. As a result, 3M doesn't lose good scientists and engineers only to gain poor managers, a common problem in the manufacturing sector. (Govindarajan and Srinivas 2013)*

Behavior: Has High Technical Expertise

It is important for your credibility as a leader to have technical expertise in at least one area related to your organization's work. It is not essential that you be an expert in all the fields in which your leadership team has specialties. You do not have to be an expert accountant, expert marketing specialist, expert production person. For the areas in which you do not have expertise, it is important to ask critical questions of your staff members. For example:

> What might be missing from what you are telling me?
> How does this interface with the other functional areas in the company?

➤ With whom did you consult to help you articulate this advice you are giving me?

➤ If you were me, what would you be hesitant about?

➤ What risk is involved?

When I was at the Yale School of Management getting my MBA, I remember a professor saying, "We don't teach you the answers. We teach you how to ask the right questions."

Behavior: Has High Cognitive Intelligence

Intelligence is a complex topic, and the concept is going through major rethinking because of new research about how the brain functions, and all the different ways people have to express a wide range of intellectual capabilities.

"Generally speaking, cognitive intelligence refers to the ability to reason, mentally focus, process visual information and have a working memory. For example, when we talk about IQ, we mean cognitive intelligence" (Hlebowitsh 2021). But IQ as a measure of someone's intellectual ability has concerning limitations, as David Berg, clinical professor and lecturer in psychiatry at Yale University, points out:

> *The history of conceptualizing and measuring intelligence is so fraught with the obvious problem of social construction that I find it both not useful and evocative of supremacy and exploitation (in which the concept was enlisted for generations . . . and still is). Given the work on "multiple intelligences" (a step in the right direction) and your previous statements about complementarity in leadership (a concept you know is near and dear to my professional heart) I'm not sure why you need some general concept of cognitive ability. You could just describe the elements and leave out the general (g) nomenclature or re-emphasize (as I do in my paper on leadership and followership) that it is the complementarity that is important. Given the different abilities required for leadership in different fields, the diversity of phenotypes in leadership roles and the shaky nature of the whole concept of general intelligence, I think it is a slim reed to stand on. (David Berg, personal communication, January 5, 2023)*

TABLE 7.1   Fluid Versus Crystallized Intelligence

Fluid Intelligence	Crystallized Intelligence
New information	Stored information
Short-term memory	Long-term memory
Increases through childhood, peaks at adolescence, then declines	Increases through childhood, and slows with aging, then stabilizes or continues to increase throughout life
Functions include working memory, processing speed, reasoning, cognitive control, inhibition, complex skills, attention tasks, creativity	Functions include procedural (practical), declarative (factual), general and specialized knowledge, wisdom

SOURCE: https://psychcentral.com/lib/what-is-emotional-intelligence-eq. Last accessed February 15, 2023.

One new way of thinking about types of intelligence is fluid intelligence and crystallized intelligence (Figure 7.1). Crystallized intelligence encompasses the older concept of technical or content expertise; fluid intelligence encompasses and improves on the older competence of IQ.

OPG is redoing the research that is the foundation of the Abundance Leadership model, as is good practice with any model. I anticipate that this particular behavior—cognitive intelligence—will be transformed. When we are redoing the research, we will engage with researchers in the fields of psychology, neuroscience, and other areas that can help us develop a more nuanced leadership behavior related to this skill set.

Tips and Activities for Creativity

- Always ask "Why not?" when a creative solution appears; see Barry Nalebuff and Ian Ayers' (2003) book, *Why Not? How to Use Everyday Ingenuity to Solve Problems Big and Small.*
- Use a variety of facilitation techniques to elicit creative ideas from your staff members.
- Say yes more often.
- Create spaces and funds for creativity, with no metrics or goals or due dates or expectations.
- Use *and* instead of *but* when reacting to an idea.

CHAPTER 8

Visibility

More visibility is more power, but more vulnerability.

—Ezra Furman

Meta-Competency	Competency	Abundance Behavior
Visibility	Visibility	Manages by walking around; is visible to staff members
		Does not hide in their office; maximizes contact with others

Visibility is a critical abundance leadership habit; it assuages our staff members' subconscious fears about the loss of a leader. It also tells the staff members that you are present and accounted for, are aware of what the tenor of the organization is, and more.

A few years ago, I had a coaching client who was a high introvert and was trained in accounting, a profession that lends itself to more solitary-type work. He was leading a team of about 15 staff members involved in finance and accounting. He wanted to become a more accessible and visible leader and asked me for some advice on techniques to do so. I suggested to him that every morning he take the time to say hello to each staff member and check in with them, whenever he had the time.

I also recommended that he keep a list of all his staff members' names on a sheet on his desk and each week put a check mark next to those with whom he had interacted one-on-one. This is a good way to make sure you are connecting with all your staff members and also that you are not favoring one over another to an inappropriate extent.

Rob Barber, an Abundance Leadership Program alumni, shared this insight about visibility: "Visibility was key—especially during COVID when we worked remotely. I had to rethink ways to be 'visible' and connected to my team. While I would typically walk around to connect with folks—instead—I had to identify other strategies to connect . . . standing morning check-in meetings, 'office hours' for staff to utilize via Zoom and then plan for the next phase hybrid work (i.e., what meetings needed to return to in-person; who struggled during remote and would most benefit from in-office during a staff reduction period, etc.)."

Is visibility just being physically visible to others? Physical visibility alone doesn't scratch the surface of the impact of true visibility, with all its components. Highly visible leaders create more trust. They also foster greater independence and a greater sense of well-being among employees. The visibility competency cluster has two closely intertwined behaviors: "Manages by walking around; is visible to staff members" and "Does not hide in their office; maximizes contact with others."

Visibility includes these qualities:

➤ Being accessible, available, and present
➤ Knowing what the team is working on, and letting them know what you are working on
➤ Modeling good leadership practices and transparency
➤ Gaining recognition for the leader's and the team's work

Visible leaders are often available leaders. Available leaders put team members and colleagues on their list of priorities, leave time in their weekly calendar for unscheduled conversations, and make clear to others how and when they can be reached. Visible leaders also keep their meeting commitments as best they can and make good use of technology—particularly videoconferencing—to be available virtually when they cannot be physically (adapted from "The Leadership Difference Between Being Accessible and Available," https://eblingroup.com/blog/accessible-and-available/).

Here is an example of powerful visibility: at OPG, our calendars are completely visible to one another. Staff members can choose to keep their work and personal calendars separate or in one blended calendar, using "private" to keep personal appointments not visible. As a partner, I use one calendar and rarely make even personal activities private so the staff members can see how and when they can rely on me.

As another example of the power of visibility, over 20 years ago, a client of mine, a CEO who ran a group of magazines, told me that he would often go down to the loading docks to smoke. He said he learned more about what was, or was not, working in his organization on the loading docks than he did in many of his leadership team meetings.

Tips and Activities for Visibility

- ➤ Move your body out of your office, through the halls, onto the loading docks, into the soul of your organization.
- ➤ Engage in the simple and critical work of making the human connection. Say hello. Stop to talk to people.
- ➤ Repeat what is important for the organization's survival, over and over.
- ➤ Hold open office hours.
- ➤ Make your calendar visible to staff members.
- ➤ Rotate through your direct reports' staff meetings.

CHAPTER 9

Self-Awareness

The most powerful relationship you will ever have is the relationship with yourself.

—Steve Maraboli

Meta-Competency	Competency	Abundance Behavior
Self-Awareness	Reflection and affect	Seeks out the opinion and energy of others when appropriate
		Is rarely ruffled and keeps an even tone and affect in most situations
		Manages their time well
	Interpersonal adeptness	Demonstrates empathy and compassion for others
		Gives their attention and kindness without effort
		Addresses conflict
	Morality	Has a strong moral compass that is evident in their language and actions
		Is trustworthy
	Ego control	Is humble
		Is not egocentric; does not have a "me, me" attitude

"I've decided to step down from my leadership role and go back to teaching."

"I don't want to be the head of IT anymore; I miss the coding and design work I used to do before I became a leader."

These are rare but not unheard-of comments from some of Tony's and my coaching clients. "Why is this so darn hard?!" is a frequent lament we hear in managers' and leaders' offices. Managing and leading are not easy. Is one or all of the following true for you on a regular basis?

- Managing is exhausting you.
- Managing is exciting you.
- Leading is scaring you.
- Leading is thrilling you.

Based on my experience teaching thousands of managers and leaders, I estimate that only 10% of people are natural managers and leaders. Often it is the lure of higher compensation or more status that causes people to say yes to managing and leading. Only later do they realize that they have left behind the very activities and content that made them happy in their field. The accountant no longer balances books; as a leader, they spend all day in meetings on strategy and performance reviews. The architect no longer designs building; instead they spend their days reviewing budgets and interviewing job applicants.

Before taking on a management or leadership role, ask yourself if you really want not only the psychological load of leading and managing, but also the daily content. As Annie Dillard, the writer, said, "How we spend our days is of course how we spend our lives" (2013). Will the daily tasks involved in leading and managing be fulfilling? It is okay to say no. Our culture sees leadership as a sign of success and there is usually a significant salary bump; this makes it hard to say no.

Figures 9.1 and 9.2 show the changes in focus and needed skill sets we experience as we move from being a content contributor to manager to leader. We need less of our original professional expertise and more interpersonal and managerial skills. We must seek out training in these skills because they are rarely provided in our professional credential training. MDs don't take accounting courses. Accountants don't take performance management courses.

Ninety percent or more of your work as a leader is with people. What really matters now is your ability to work *with* people and manage yourself. To do this better, the greatest gift you can give others is self-awareness—awareness of how you come off, what your triggers are, what matters to you, what you love, and what you dislike. Abundance Leadership alumni put self-awareness at the top of their list of most-used meta-competencies. One test for your level of self-awareness is

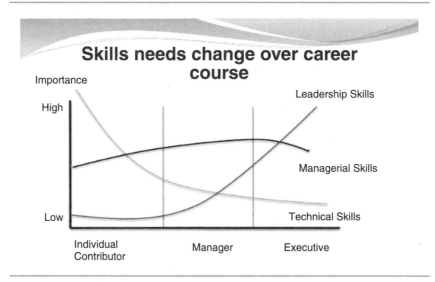

FIGURE 9.1   Change in focus as we move to leading.

SOURCE: Dr. Win Maug.

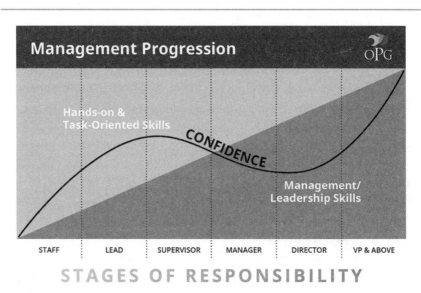

FIGURE 9.2   The management progression shows how we leave behind our content skills the higher up we go in an organization.

SOURCE: OPG/Tony Panos.

how surprised you are when you hear critical feedback. As one of my professors once said, "After a certain age, if you are surprised by the feedback, you haven't been listening."

I would add that you haven't been doing the work. Self-awareness takes work. It can be exhausting, but the benefits are enormous. This work is particularly important because leaders are watched, a lot. Your staff members are acutely aware of your affect, and small gestures are magnified because of what I call "the iconic power of position." Your title gives you power and influence to an exponential degree. For example, a small passing remark on your part can be overinterpreted and create a shift in the culture.

One aspect of being a good leader is learning to be bigger, better, and different than the self or behaviors to which you might naturally default. The art of abundant, authentic leadership is bringing your true, well-curated self to work as often as possible so that your leadership has a positive impact on people, on achieving your organization's purpose, and on the world.

The more self-aware you become, the more you are in full choice in every aspect of your life. Self-awareness is often focused on changing problematic behaviors but it can be even more powerful when it is used to affirm strengths *and* to enable you to use problematic behaviors in better ways.

One thought on authenticity in the workplace, which is related to self-awareness—I think there is and should be a difference between the professional authenticity we exhibit at work versus the personal authenticity we exhibit at home or other settings. I do not think it is appropriate to do or say or wear anything you feel like in a work setting. Old school to some extent.

At OPG, we often say to our clients, "You get paid too much to be yourself." What do we mean? Always work toward reducing how and when you inflict your hurtful, counterproductive behaviors on others. At the top of the organizational food chain, you can get away with all kinds of bad and hurtful behaviors because no one can risk being fully honest with you. Self-awareness might not eliminate all your less helpful behaviors, but it will help you reduce their frequency of appearance and enable you to talk about them when they come up.

Be sure you have a safe person and place with whom you can vent without filtering. It's important to allow yourself some time to get the feelings and fears out.

"We do not learn from experience. . . . We learn from reflecting on experience."

—John Dewey

REFLECTION AND AFFECT

If we are self-aware, we can learn and change, which in turn enables our organizations to learn and change. We can serve as role models for staff members and make it possible for people to share their insights into themselves in ways that help them, their colleagues, and the organization grow.

One Abundance Leadership alumni shared that "currently reflection and affect are in high-use mode in my leadership approach. We've had a number of controversial discussions and reasons for individuals to take lots of decisions personally. In order to remain effective, and have my own perspective heard, I have had to really remain calm, use positive language, and monitor the room before speaking about topics that I am passionate about and are going differently than I think they should."

The Abundance Leadership model has a few behaviors that help increase your self-awareness.

Behavior: Seeks Out the Opinion and Energy of Others When Appropriate

Reflection is the habit and ability of stopping to think about what you have done or how you have appeared to others. This habit can also include getting feedback from others, watching oneself on video, or listening to oneself on a taped conversation. This is a difficult practice because it can be hard to see how we appear to others, especially if we are working on our gravitas and power.

There can be an overemphasis on being nice as a leader. Finding that balance between expressing direction, power, and opinions with being open and listening is hard. I go back to something I mentioned in the Preface: I don't think your goal is to have everyone like you. For those with whom you are really not a good fit, it is best if they are not directly reporting to you or are not in your organization if they are highly problematic. It is okay to surround yourself with people with whom you have a good interpersonal flow.

Reflecting on your affect, affect being how one comes off to others, is a good habit, but choose what you want to work on and what you want to keep about yourself. No one is asking you to be perfect; just be your best compassionate self. What are some signs of knowing ourselves?

- Being able to name the main qualities that make you you
- Having a clear sense of your core values and your priorities
- Knowing what you like and don't like
- Identifying what makes you feel comfortable and uncomfortable
- Acknowledging what you are willing and not willing to do
- Being aware of how you are likely to react or are reacting in a given situation (think reflection)

These qualities, along with your vision and values for leading, build confidence and ease in engaging and being transparent.

Here are some questions Tony Panos, a partner at OPG, uses to help his coaching clients reflect on an experience:

- What did we learn from this experience? About what we did? About us?
- What is worth repeating about this experience? What should we try to avoid?
- How will this experience affect what we believe in? Our cause? Our purpose?
- If we went through this experience again, what would we do differently?
- What did we learn about our assumptions going into this experience? How should that influence our future assumptions?

Behavior: Is Rarely Ruffled and Keeps an Even Tone and Affect in Most Situations

There is a risk with overmanaging your affect and emotions (both verbal and nonverbal). If you and your staff members become artificially upbeat and emotionally monochromatic, it will be hard to have teams fully trust one another and to develop high levels of productivity and communication. Determining which emotions are acceptable at work, and to what extent, should be an ongoing conversation with your staff. Arlie Hochschild, a professor at UC Berkeley, wrote a book called *The Managed Heart*, which looks at the impact on staff members of professions in which emotions are dictated, professions such as airline attendants, call center operators, nurses, and others. As described on Blinkist, *"The Managed Heart* is the seminal sociological text that introduced the concept of emotional labor" (https://www.blinkist.com/en/books/the-managed-heart-en). (See Figure 9.3.)

> ". . . leaders who emit the negative register—who are irritable, touchy, domineering, cold—repel people. No one wants to work for a grouch. Research has proven it: Optimistic, enthusiastic leaders more easily retain their people, compared with those bosses who tend toward negative moods." (McKee 2018)

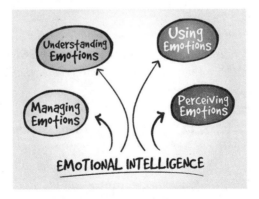

FIGURE 9.3   Elements of emotional intelligence.

SOURCE: https://www.prdaily.com/how-communicators-can-bolster-workplace-emotional-intelligence/.

Nonverbal manifestations of emotions and mood states speak loudly about your state of mind and what you are truly thinking. These manifestations can serve you well or not so well. As an Abundance Leadership alum put it, "I recognized that there were organizational issues when discussing situations with others and watching their negative body language in response."

Body language matters. As we have all experienced, another person's tone, facial expressions, and gestures convey an extraordinary array and depth of attitudes and feelings. Nonverbal cues have over four times the impact on the impression you make than anything you say (Goman, 2018).

Here are some ways to adjust your nonverbal cues:

➤ Adjust your attitude.
➤ Smile, and make eye contact.
➤ Mind your posture, and how you use your hands.
➤ A variety of hand gestures are received as warm, agreeable, and energetic; anything in excess, however, can be a negative.

Anger is a common emotion both inside and outside organizational life. It is sometimes referred to as a secondary emotion, one that is masking another emotion such as shame or fear. But Pema Chodron, the well-known Buddhist nun and teacher, notes that anger is also a powerful indicator that something is off. In the film *The Upside of Anger*, one of the characters affirms the power of anger to transform us:

> *Anger and resentment can stop you in your tracks. That's what I know now. It needs nothing to burn but the air and the life that it swallows and smothers. It's real, though—the fury, even when it isn't. It can change you . . . turn you . . . mold you and shape you into something you're not. The only upside to anger, then . . . is the person you become. Hopefully someone that wakes up one day and realizes they're not afraid to take the journey, someone that knows that the truth is, at best, a partially told story. That anger, like growth, comes in spurts and fits, and in its wake, leaves a new chance at acceptance, and the promise of calm. Then again, what do I know? I'm only a child.*
>
> Lavender Popeye Wolfmeyer (played by Evan
> Rachel Wood); from the script by Michael
> Binder for the movie *The Upside of Anger*

Here are four tips for leaders for dealing with employee emotions, paraphrased from a blogpost by Jocelyn Stange on Quantumworkplace.com:

Regardless of how well you handle your own emotions, you can't control the emotions of others. But it is important to learn how to acknowledge them and respond appropriately. Unresolved issues can lead to decreased productivity, damaged relationships, and lowered engagement.

Allow for Mistakes

No one is perfect—plain and simple. Mistakes are inevitable and, although they don't need to be simply accepted, they also aren't grounds for a scolding. Berating or punishing employees can cause humiliation and hostility.

Calmly correcting or excusing the rare mistake is a great way to build trust. In fact, helping reduce negative emotions with transparency, open communication, and authenticity will lead to better relationships with your employees. But if mistakes continue to pile up, you should schedule time with your employees to create a performance improvement plan. This plan will help make sure both parties are on the same page and set clear expectations for success.

Build a Culture of Trust

Sharing emotions, especially uncomfortable ones, is one way to show vulnerability. But we can't be vulnerable if we don't trust the people that we're sharing our stories with. Everyone in your organization should feel comfortable being themselves and expressing their emotions.

It's not enough just to let employees know they can share their feelings—you must be willing to be the example, too. When employees can witness a culture of honesty and compassion, they'll be able to understand and adapt to others' emotions.

Be Present

When managers and leaders are unavailable, employees may feel anxious and undervalued. Make time to connect with your team to instill confidence in your employees, their work, and their performance. Empowering your team members to stay connected in this way helps build positive relationships.

Set uninterrupted time apart for each employee at least once a month. And if you're really committed to the cause, we recommend meeting once a week—even for a quick check-in. These meetings offer employees an opportunity to ask questions, provide updates, raise concerns, and provide feedback. These are perfect times to celebrate successes to increase positive emotions in the workplace.

Listen More Than You Talk

Most times, employees who experience negative emotions aren't searching for solutions. They want to express themselves and release their pent-up emotions. Listening to your employees allows them to get it all out there and makes them feel cared for and heard. It also establishes you as a trusted resource who can be depended on.

When dealing with someone else's emotions, strive to understand what they are feeling and why. Ask them how they are feeling and if they are okay. If they don't want to talk or say everything is fine, respect their wishes and don't pressure them any further. If they do want to talk it out, find a quiet space and listen.

Your employees are only human, and humans are emotional creatures. Addressing emotions is important for recognizing your employees for who they are and improving your emotional culture.

Understanding and managing the emotions of your employees at work is only the first step. Use these tips to guide your engagement efforts and bring humanity back to the workplace. (Stange 2021)

Tony Panos adds to these tips: "If an employee says they're fine but you think this is not the case, consider stating what you observed in their behavior and ask if your perception, and the meaning you assigned to it, is correct."

Here are some questions to help you manage emotions and affect:

➤ Do I consider how my response will influence others?
➤ Does showing emotion in this situation help me obtain my objective?

> Am I equipped to deal with unexpected stress?
> Do I consider what I say or how I behave before responding to a situation? Did I prepare?
> What strategies can I use to regulate my emotions? Am I using tools like mindful meditation to help me control my emotions in the long term?

I would encourage you to examine your underlying paradigm about life. How do you react when you hit a traffic jam? What is your reaction when you have missed the plane? What do you do when you don't make a sale? Or when an employee leaves who was a critical part of the team? How do you process difficulty and change? I often say to my son, "If you don't like chores and errands, life is going to be a real drag." The point here is to find joy or at least calmness in the midst of irritations, disruptions, and delays.

"In social interactions others' feelings, as they may be observed from others' verbal and nonverbal communication, may convey information that influences the further course of the interaction."

—*Keltner and Haidt (1999)*

Your mental model matters in managing emotions. The steps to having a healthy mental model include (1) awareness of your existing mental model's strengths and challenges, (2) transforming your mental model through active interruption of problematic habits and behaviors that are driven by your old mental model, and (3) sustained use of a new mental model as a driver for more productive behaviors and relationships.

Tips and Activities for Managing Emotions

> Understand the value of emotions.
> Be prepared for events with high stress or tension.
> Take your time; respond rather than react.
> Focus on what you can control.
> Engage in mindfulness practice (a mental state achieved by focusing one's awareness on the present moment while calmly acknowledging and accepting one's feelings, thoughts, and body sensations).

> ➤ Remember that expectations are resentments under construction.
> ➤ Practice psychosynthesis. (See the next section on "Manages Their Time Well" for more on psychosynthesis.)

Behavior: Manages Their Time Well

As a leader, there are high demands on your time and attention. If these demands are not managed well, through good time management and delegation, you, like all people, will start to show signs of stress. This in turn leads to behaving in ways that a scarcity leader behaves—being unsettled, making decisions in ways that do not empower your staff members, and more.

There is a great deal written about how to manage your time. I leave you to discover those books and ideas on your own. I do want to mention a few techniques and ideas that we have at OPG about managing time well. Some of these are tactical, some are psychological, and some are philosophical.

In one of the time management workshops that I teach, I use a framework called the 4 Ds: do, delegate, delay, and drop. I ask people to take out both their personal and professional to-do lists and sort them into the 4 Ds. Most people find it difficult to take anything out of the do category and move it into one of the other three. I recommend that instead of trying to drop something from the do list, people put it in the delay list. It seems to be easier to postpone something than to say no to it. And yet a few months later, the delayed item has often disappeared from the list completely. Magic!

The 4 Ds

- ➤ Do
- ➤ Delegate (up, down, across, and outside of your organization or department)
- ➤ Delay
- ➤ Drop

It is a little bit like the habit I have of doing the house document filing only once a year. I find that if I wait long enough most of the papers that I thought were important to keep, have become completely irrelevant and go into the shredder.

I taught this workshop at Yale once to a group of women faculty members. At the end of the workshop, a woman in her late 70s or possibly early 80s came up to me and said, "I decided not to write another book as a result of this workshop. I have decided to spend more time with my husband." I remember thinking that the university leadership wouldn't be so thrilled with that decision but it was brilliant on her part. She had weighed the gain of writing another book, one of many she had written in her lifetime, versus more quality time with her husband, who was also getting older.

Most of all, do not raise your hand; do not volunteer to help when you are overloaded.

Leading takes intentionality, effort, and practice. You need to show up for yourself first, which means taking care of your physical and mental health and being kind to yourself. It also means setting boundaries, saying no to some demands. By showing up for ourselves, we can avoid resentment, one-sided relationships, and burnout. An Abundance Leadership alumni noted, the model "changed my personal life as I became a more active family member recognizing that it is acceptable to say no to meetings. I took better control of my schedule." And another shared, "It has improved my personal relationships."

Your prime directive in any situation is to take care of yourself. Self-care is a prerequisite for organizational health; you are the primary source of balance, direction, vision, and energy for your group. There is a direct correlation between your organization's success and your well-being—never doubt it.

Self-care is also inextricably linked to time management. I don't think this is a profound insight and yet it seems very hard for leaders and others to incorporate significant self-care into their lives. I do not need to state the obvious that texting, emails, and other potentially invasive forms of communication have made it almost impossible to go offline for any significant period of time. It takes enormous self-control to turn off the alerts, the beeps, the pop-ups. Yet my clients will tell me that more exercise, more sleep, better food, more time with family, and more downtime radically increase their productivity.

Oxygen and the air pressure are always being monitored. In the event of a decompression, an oxygen mask will automatically appear in front of you. To start the flow of oxygen, pull the mask toward you. Place it firmly over your nose and mouth, secure the elastic band behind your head, and breathe normally. Although the bag does not inflate, oxygen is flowing to the mask. If you are traveling with a child or someone who requires assistance, secure your mask on first, and then assist the other person. Keep your mask on until a uniformed crew member advises you to remove it. (https://airodyssey.net/reference/inflight/#safety)

The list of reasons our clients give us as to why they cannot improve their self-care and work–life balance is long and frankly sometimes tedious to listen to. It is as if they have abdicated all control over their lives.

- "Once this project is done, I'll start working out again."
- "If I don't work 90 hours a week, then my staff members won't."
- "I'm too busy at home to exercise."
- "I can't say no to _____." *(fill in the blank)*

A common underlying driver of overworked leaders and staff members is inadequate staffing. I have advised my higher education leaders to have an algorithm that shows how many additional physical, human, and technological resources are needed every time a faculty member is hired. This is rarely calculated, and without it both the existing staff and the new faculty member feel short-changed.

Here's another example of the need for an algorithm. At Yale, the clerical and technical staff members used to get about two months off a year, including all holidays and PTO. That means that for every five clerical and technical staff members, you need a sixth one to cover the time off. Have you asked your HR leadership to make similar calculations? Have you thought about what that algorithm might look like for your job?

If you truly cannot find your way to take better care of yourself and create better balance in your life, it might be time to see a counselor.

Here are a few other tips that might help you with time management and overload that we try our best to practice at OPG. Most of these you will have heard of before. I share these to encourage you to try them, knowing that we are trying them in our firm and having some success with them.

First put in transition time between meetings. Shorten meetings to 45 or 50 minutes. I recommend starting meetings on the hour and ending at 45 minutes past or 50 minutes past the hour. We color code transition time in our calendars so we are aware that it is there. After I teach a workshop, I usually have at least an hour of transition time so I do not have to leave the room too quickly and can linger with workshop participants and help the staff members pack up the room. Giving yourself adequate transition time allows for traffic and parking problems, problems finding a room, and other problems to occur without them derailing you. You can arrive more relaxed and more centered.

As I discuss in Chapter 5, we also have a four-day workweek, which is helpful for ensuring that household matters can be taken care of on Fridays, and then Saturdays and Sundays have more relaxation and downtime in them.

Another tip, obvious to many, is to turn off all alerts coming from emails, texts, and other sources of overload and distraction. In some professions it is not possible to turn off alerts, but you might try turning off these alerts for an hour or so. We do ask our staff members to keep their phones on silent as much as possible, with the exception of when family and children and emergencies might need attending to.

I want to also share two habits that are profoundly detrimental to human beings—especially managers, leaders, and those around them—monkey mind and comparative mind.

Monkey Mind

Zen Buddhists refer to the constant chatter of the mind as monkey mind. The Buddha held that the human mind is filled with drunken monkeys flinging themselves from tree branches, jumping around, and chattering nonstop. He meant that our minds

*are in constant motion. Typical mind chatter sounds like the
following:*

- ➤ *Your mind making a laundry list of to-do items*
- ➤ *Your mind listing its fears, both real and imaginary*
- ➤ *Your mind recalling hurtful things that have happened in the
  past*
- ➤ *Your mind judging the present*
- ➤ *Your mind creating catastrophic "what-if" scenarios of the
  future (Fabrega 2022)*

One mental model that helps people reduce the monkey mind chatter is "spheres of influence" thinking—focusing on what you can control so you can have greater influence (Figure 9.4). You will improve your opportunity to influence outcomes by focusing on what you can control—yourself. That means focusing on you, your choices, and your reactions to events and people.

Focus to a lesser extent on what you can influence. Avoid focusing on what you cannot control or influence. As much as we would like to, we cannot control other people's thoughts or feelings.

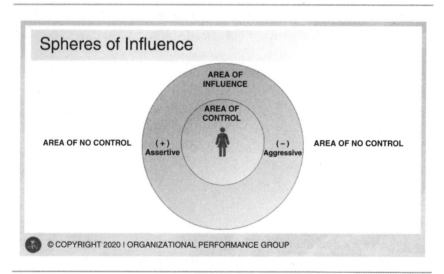

FIGURE 9.4   Spheres of influence.

SOURCE: Adapted from the work of Mary D'Amato by Anthony Panos.

The second concept that helps improve our self-awareness, confidence, and self-worth is comparative mind.

Comparative Mind

We live in a very competitive culture where status is determined by who has the most money, who won the game or the argument. We are also plagued by self-criticism, often judging our life experiences unmercifully. These mental states generate much suffering. (Carlson and Crawford 2011)

Comparative mind contributes to our pain and imbalance, which has an impact on our ability to be abundance leaders. The thoughts associated with comparative mind often sound like the following:

- "She's got more money than I do."
- "I didn't do enough today."
- "Why can't I get grades as good as they get?"
- "I'm not as thin as that person."

And on and on it goes—the mind in full negation of the moment and the beauty of what is right now. The problem with this thinking is that it detracts from self-confidence, takes your eye off the present moment and the possibility of enjoying that moment, and takes you out of your own immediate experience. Comparative mind also creates aggression and fear.

The comparative mind and its ally, the critical judgmental voice, constantly tell us that we are not good enough in so many ways. The critical judgment voice is related to the comparative mind, but it is even more than just comparison. It is the voice of our mean teachers, our overly critical parents, the bullies in the school yard, and the images in the media. It is the voice that says you are not good enough, you are not thin enough, how could you have done that?! What were you thinking?! Look at you, you always make that mistake!

This voice can be relentless and painful. It keeps us out of living fully in our own bodies, in our own heart and soul, in the present moment, and from an abundance orientation. Our entire life can go by spent worried about what we did in the past and what we should be doing in the future, instead of living deeply in our current breath and in the beauty that surrounds us, and in our own "perfect imperfections," as John Legend says.

I want to introduce you to a profoundly transformative practice that comes from the psychological tradition of psychosynthesis. I call this practice psychosynthesis, but it is only one practice from the broader psychological approach known as psychosynthesis. "Psychosynthesis, a transpersonal psychology and therapeutic approach, offers such a model of the human personality, in which the psychological and spiritual perspectives can converge" (Lombard 2017).

For this moment, I will just refer to this practice as psychosynthesis. It is the practice of reviewing your day at the end of the day as if you were watching a movie. You play the day back and narrate it, avoiding adjectives, adverbs, criticism, and judgment.

Here is what the narration usually sounds like when we review our day with the critical voice turned up to full volume, *not* using the psychosynthesis method.

> *I woke up late this morning, after turning off the alarm seven times. I don't know why I'm so lazy. I went downstairs and fed the dogs, and I gave Spot too much food. It's my fault that he has gained so much weight because I do not take him out for walks enough. I made breakfast and I put too much sugar in my coffee. I then went back upstairs to take a shower and left the water running for too long. I'm really hurting the environment.*

You can hear the judgment in this narration. Now let's try it with removing the judgment.

> *I woke up this morning. The alarm rang 7 times. I went downstairs and fed the dogs. I gave Spot two cups of food and Neptune one cup of food. I made coffee and put 4 teaspoons of sugar in my coffee. I went back upstairs and ran the water for 10 minutes to warm it up, and then I took a shower.*

I encourage you to try this practice at the end of your day for about six to eight weeks. Even if you do it three times a week for six weeks, you will start to feel a difference in how you treat yourself internally. I have used this practice for over 30 years, and it has freed me from almost all self-criticism. Hurtful self-criticism runs counter to an abundance mental model. Kindness toward yourself is an essential practice for leading abundantly. When something goes awry or I could have done something differently, I do not have a judgmental, mean voice internally anymore. I say, "Next time I'll do it differently."

Tips and Activities for Reflection and Affect

- Meditate.
- Go to counseling.
- Talk to yourself in the mirror.
- Keep a journal.
- As comparative mind arises, notice the comparisons and let them float away.
- Acknowledge what is great about right now.
- Practice the 4 Ds: do, delegate, drop, delay.
- Recognize aggression as a sign that you are trying to control something you cannot.
- Be assertive; it helps build influence.
- Ask for feedback on your affect. Be sure to state your interest in doing so.
- Use your 360-degree feedback report on a biannual basis.
- Get a coach or use colleagues at work to assist with reflection.
- Practice psychosynthesis debriefing of the day.

INTERPERSONAL ADEPTNESS

Abundance leaders inspire their staff members through many means, one of which is interpersonal interaction. For some people, interaction with others comes easily. Extroverts tend to be more likely to do so with ease. For others, such as high introverts, interacting with others, with ease and adeptness, takes practice (and can require periods of alone time to recover). Whether an extrovert or introvert, interpersonal adeptness can be learned through practice.

Behaviors: (1) Demonstrates Empathy and Compassion for Others and (2) Gives Their Attention and Kindness Without Effort

These behaviors are hard to exhibit when we are in a rush or if we feel some people are more worthy of our attention than others. When I was the director of OD at Yale, I was at a work reception at Yale, speaking with a leader. As we were talking, I noticed that his eyes kept darting around the room, particularly to the door. As soon as someone higher up than him arrived, he walked away from our conversation mid-sentence. This is the opposite of giving attention without effort.

I encourage you to notice what is distracting you from focusing on the person in front of you. If it is time, and you want to give them your full attention, acknowledge this and let them know you'll be back. If you are distracted because you are overly focused on power dynamics, I encourage you to remember what this would feel like if you were the one not being listened to fully.

At OPG, we teach a detailed and difficult method of listening deeply called *active listening*. In this method, one of the first steps is to create what my sister, Maria, calls *good local conditions* (as opposed to *lousy local conditions*). In other words, make sure you have the time and the right physical location, and also that the person is ready to share.

Behavior: Addressed Conflict

Abundance leaders see conflict as opportunity and information.

Conflict is healthy and ever present in almost every situation in which we are interacting with other people. Conflict can be so mild as to be about what you will eat for dinner. Or it can be so extreme that we are at war with one another. All along that spectrum are millions of moments of low-, high-, or medium-level conflict.

We choose to navigate conflict in different ways all day long. We make those choices based on our physical health, mental health, our training in conflict management, our desired outcomes, and so many more factors. Which conflict do we choose to engage in? Which conflict do we choose to walk away from?

The author Edward Abbey, said, "What's the truth? I don't know and I'm sorry I brought it up." This thought underlies all of my approaches to conflict resolution. There are always multiple truths at play in any situation. The facts. The facts as I see them. The facts as you see them. My truth of my feelings. Your truth of your feelings.

Choosing to work through conflict with someone takes skills, courage, and commitment to the relationship. It is an investment in the relationship, an act of deepening the connection between you and them. It is an expression of respect and valuing the other person. It takes time and energy, so it is important to choose with whom you resolve conflict.

I think sometimes people confuse asking for what they need with conflict. Asking for what you need is not conflict. Do your best to ask for what you need in a timely manner without aggression or negative affect. Practice in the mirror. Write out a script. Practice with your dog. Practice with a trusted colleague.

Are you a person who is afraid to resolve conflict to the point that you are leaving relationships behind that you have valued, or are you not furthering critical relationships? Are you avoiding discussing your needs, feelings, and reactions to interactions with someone to the point that you have begun to keep a list or spin an alternative narrative?

Are you a person who keeps lists of grievances about others? This is a sure sign that you are having problems resolving conflict or you are in 'wrong relationship' with someone in your life. What do I mean by wrong relationship? Sometimes we are in a relationship with someone as a friend, for example, when in truth we would be better off with this person as a professional colleague. Maybe you are married to someone with whom you would be in 'right relationship' if they were a friend instead of your spouse.

Finding the right relationship with each person and resolving conflict immediately can create wonderful relationships. Of course, there are some people with whom we should not be in any relationship. They are abusive no matter what relationship they have with us or they just are not a good fit with who we are at our core. Or maybe they are unreliable or behave in an inconsistent way. Remember that sometimes when a relationship breaks apart, it is a great gift to you.

One of the Abundance Leadership Immersion Program alumni overcame their reticence to resolve conflict with a staff member and saw great benefits as a result. The alumni discovered that not only did they resolve the problem, but they also strengthened their relationship with the staff member.

Let's look at another aspect of conflict in organizations. When a problem arises, it is human nature to try to determine who is to blame, to look for an individual to target. If we can just get rid of so-and-so, everything will be better. The problem with this thinking is that it misses the source of a majority of an organization's (and society's) problems, and it is a manifestation of a judging mindset. (See Chapter 10 on communication for more on judging mindsets.)

Problems originate at many levels in a system: individual, group, department, organization, nation, planet (see Figure 9.5). Sometimes the problem is the system. Sometimes it's the individual, but it might be that the individual's problematic behavior is the result of system failure.

Based on our experience at OPG, a majority of the time, some aspect of all problems originates from a *systemic* failure, bottleneck, glitch,

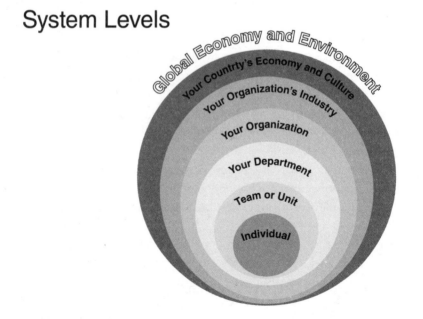

FIGURE 9.5   System embeddedness.

SOURCE: Laura Freebairn-Smith (Author).

process, or rule. So why don't we spend more time fixing the system? It's hard work. In the short term, it's easier to blame the individual and move on. Surprise! The problem keeps showing up in the form of the next "problem employee" because you haven't fixed the systemic issue.

System work takes a long time and lots of discussion. Once in a while, you get lucky and you can fix the system quickly but be prepared to spend more time on system-wide solutions. Instead of assuming an employee who is struggling is not a fit anywhere in your organization, consider that all weeds are flowers in the wrong place. Where can that person become a flower in your organization or in another organization?

As always, get help with conflict resolution. Mentoring, training, and other forms of support critical in this particular aspect of leading.

Here are some questions to consider when you look around and try to find out who is at fault for a problem:

➤ Why am I only focusing on the individual? What might be happening in the larger system or context that is producing this situation?
➤ What's the psychological contract at play here for everyone? What rights and responsibilities are appropriate for each of us to have in this situation?
➤ Does this problem keep recurring, despite our best efforts to fix it?
➤ What boundaries are in play? What is appropriate behavior? Appropriate degrees of connection?
➤ What data might I be missing?

Tips and Activities for Interpersonal Adeptness

➤ Be aware of the impact of your nonverbal signals (facial expressions, body position, etc.).
➤ Stay focused and be present. Give your attention to the people with whom you are interacting.
➤ Connect with your emotions; know when they are in play.
➤ Resolve conflict in a timely manner; it is an act of respect and commitment.

> ➤ Don't ghost people or sever relationships without doing the honorable thing of explaining why.
> ➤ If you are making a list of grievances, put the mental pen down and go see the person, or ask if you are in right relationship with them.

MORALITY

Ethical behavior is doing the right thing when no one else is watching—even when doing the wrong thing is legal.

—ALDO LEOPOLD

At a meeting with a client, as we were wrapping up their strategic planning process, we got into a discussion about the difficulty of recruiting staff members at the lower levels. I asked what the pay scale was for people at the lower level, who were mostly guards and security personnel. The client said that they were paid the minimum wage. I asked, "Why?" Could the organization afford to pay more? The client replied, "Yes, but it is the market rate for those roles."

I suggested that the client might view things through a different lens. What about providing a basic livable wage? What about expressing the value of those frontline jobs by paying more? This is the kind of thinking that people look for in Abundance leaders. Why not do it differently? Do it better? Do it from a deeper place of integrity and morality?

Let's look at some specific morality-based behaviors that indicate you are an Abundance leader.

Behaviors: (1) Has a Strong Moral Compass That Is Evident in Their Language and Actions and (2) Is Trustworthy

First, the obvious—obeying the law is just a given. However, it is important to remember that the law is a de minimus standard for behavior; it is not a standard for morality, good ethics, and creating good karma.

I am not sure how much to say here. If your ethics and morality are weak or a problem, it is a nonstarter for leading from an abundance mental model. Taking the higher ground—the stronger moral ground, the better community contributor, the seventh generation thinker that

Chief Lyons encourages us to be, is not easy. Frankly a lot of the time it is a pain in the rear and it can be expensive. And yet, it allows you to go to bed at night knowing that you have done better by your staff members, by your community, and by the world.

One of the indicators of a moral person is that they recognize when they have a moral dilemma, and they seek advice. They weigh the advice and then choose a course of action. They realize that morality is not completely relative, an argument some people like to make to justify their actions. The ultimate test of whether you are on the moral high ground is whether you would want your action done to you, and what would your parents or children think.

In an inverse situation, one of the AL alumni uses their insights to manage an unethical boss: "It helped me to understand where my limits were when dealing with an immediate supervisor who is unethical and not trustworthy."

Another alumnus, when asked if the program helped improve their organization's effectiveness, shared that "indirectly, I ended up resigning my position after getting everything set for the next person. My resignation catalyzed a process at the organization wherein the unethical and ineffective leader was allowed to retire."

Tips and Activities for Morality

- Identify black, white, and gray.
- Imagine your decision and its ramifications as a newspaper headline; would you be comfortable with it?
- Golden rule versus platinum rule (John Maxwell): do unto others as they would want you to do unto them.
- Seek advice when you are faced with a moral dilemma. This is considered one of the key signs of a moral person.

EGO CONTROL

Asking for help does not mean that we are weak or incompetent. It usually indicates an advanced level of honesty and intelligence.

—ANNE WILSON SCHAEF

Ego control is a complex matter. Ego is essential to mental health; it keeps us moving forward. It helps us love ourselves. It is only when ego runs rampant that we see deep problems in leadership.

A grandstander draws attention to himself by claiming moral or intellectual authority on a particular issue. The ego's biggest problem is its inability to learn. It can't do it, because it thinks it already knows. The ego hates to admit that it's wrong almost as much as it hates to admit that it's clueless. When challenged, it goes on the defensive. If you can spot a tendency to defend your own ignorance, you have a leg up on your ego. Grandstanding is the ego's version of leadership. It manipulates strong emotions, like shame and outrage, to bully people into complying with its agenda.

To lead without ego, simply take an interest in other people and their projects. Don't use them to judge whether you're a good manager or a good person; focus on them for their own sake. For the future's sake. It is very liberating to serve others. It can also give you the strength and conviction that the ego does not afford. (Tim Eisenhauer, n.d.)

The case of Ron Johnson, a former CEO of J.C. Penney, highlights this problem. The actions of Mr. Johnson, some driven by ego, drove J.C. Penney into the ground. The Harvard Business School case on the events of 2013 shows what happened.

In April 2013, Ron Johnson (HBS '84) stepped down after just 18 months as CEO of J.C. Penney. In his brief tenure, Johnson, an acclaimed retailer respected for his innovation and success in shaping the retail image at Target and Apple, introduced dramatic departures from J.C. Penney's traditional retail approach and enacted changes quickly and simultaneously, with little market testing. Over Johnson's final 12 months as CEO, J.C. Penney shares dropped more than 50%. The case describes the environments at Target, Apple, and J.C. Penney during Johnson's tenure and how his experiences may have shaped the strategies that he implemented while CEO at J.C. Penney. (Arayandas, Margolis, and Raffaelli 2015)

There is a fine line between confidence and arrogance. Confidence and taking ownership of your successes and contributions are important. You just do not want to do so at the expense of other people's contributions. I try to use phrases such as, "I'm not sure who came up with this idea originally." "This is an idea I started and the team has brought to life."

Tips and Activities for Ego Control

➤ Give people as much credit as you can without looking disingenuous.
➤ Take credit for your work.
➤ Avoid "me, me, me" or "I, I, I" comments and contributions at meetings.

CHAPTER **10**

Managing Well

Good management is the art of making problems so
interesting and their solutions so constructive that
everyone wants to get to work and deal with them.

—PAUL HAWKEN

Meta-Competency	Competency	Abundance Behavior
Managing Well	Team building	Looks for opportunities to build teams
		Understands and articulates the role others play in the success of the team
		Delegates
		Guides and challenges employees so that they develop
	Communication	Proactively shares as much information as possible
		Seeks out feedback and receives it with openness; willingly learns from mistakes
	Protection	Protects staff from abusive conditions
		Seeks out resources and is able to gain resources for their staff members
		Maintains healthy organizational and psychological boundaries for themselves and their team°
	Decision-making	Is decisive
		Does not make inappropriately dictatorial decisions

°This behavior is not part of the original research and has been added as the model has
been applied.

In this chapter, we will take a look at several habits and tips to help you manage well. The difference between leading and managing is blurry. Usually leading lends itself more toward the visionary and strategic aspects of organizational life. Leading includes more focus on inspiring others to achieve a mission, purpose, or bigger goal. Managing is that bridge between the strategy and larger goals of the organization and getting the day-to-day work done that helps achieve the mission or purpose.

Managing is an extensive array of techniques, habits, paradigms, and other tools that you can learn and practice. I sometimes think of managing as easier to learn than leading. Leading seems to require a mental model and characterological default setting that is not intuitive for everyone. Managing can be practiced over and over and built into the fabric of your organizational life. These practices make your employees' lives better, help them be more productive, and help them grow and develop over time.

Let's look at some of those ideas and techniques to help you manage better.

TEAM BUILDING

As a leader of these staff teams, the abundance framework has helped me in setting agendas and facilitating meaningful discussions which lead to forward-looking decisions.

—ABUNDANCE LEADERSHIP IMMERSION PROGRAM ALUMNI

It is a long-standing axiom that almost all work gets done in teams, and it remains true. Developing a better understanding of how teams evolve, learning how to recognize signs of health or "dis-ease" in teams, and working on building a strong team is time well-spent. I'll introduce you to one model that we use at OPG a great deal. There are many team building models out there. Find ones that make sense to you. Blend them if needed. Most of all use the models to guide your thinking and action.

Behaviors: (1) Looks for Opportunities to Build Teams and (2) Understands and Articulates the Role Others Play in the Success of the Team

About 20 years ago, a dean of a professional school called me to ask for help. "I'm a new dean. Just took the position about eight months ago. I noticed that my faculty don't communicate with one another or have any sense of being a team," he said.

I asked him, "How often do they meet?"

"They've met four times . . . in the last 10 years."

Your team's ability to work together well (which includes meeting together) is the foundation for a healthy organization and for having a positive impact on the world, as well as hitting your organizational targets.

At OPG, we use the Drexler-Sibbet model (see Figure 10.1), both internally and with clients to help determine at which phase each team member is and where the whole team might be. One of the helpful aspects of using a team development model is it keeps your eye on the team as a whole, dynamic system, avoiding an overfocus, often negative, on one individual.

Let me walk you through the model so you can understand its nuances and how to use it with your team. There are seven phases in the Drexler-Sibbet model. At the bottom of the figure, you notice that the first half of the phases are under the umbrella of creating, where the team is forming and becoming a team. The last half of the phases are where the team is sustaining, performing and delivering on its content.

Each phase has a question that either the individual team member or the team as a whole is trying to answer or resolve. For example, in phase 1, the question is, "Why am I here?" In phase 2, the question is, "Who are you?" If you look at the model carefully, you will notice that at each phase there are different behaviors that result depending on whether the core question is resolved or unresolved.

I have clustered the seven phases into three groupings. The first grouping, which includes phases 1 and 2, are about creating an interpersonal rapport and a sense of identity and purpose. These are critical phases in the development of a team because if they are skipped,

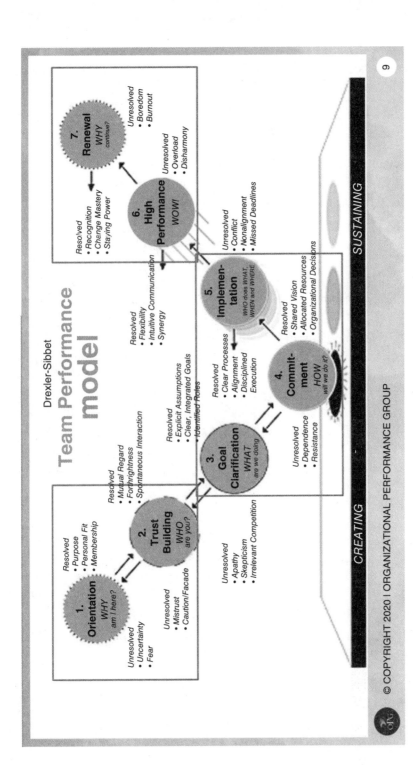

FIGURE 10.1 Drexler-Sibbet team performance model.

SOURCE: Drexler-Sibbet.

later on in the team's life, we see conflict, misalignment, and other issues arising because people do not have the interpersonal rapport necessary to resolve conflict, discuss direction, or figure out how work will get done.

The next three phases, phases 3–5, are about the work. The sequence of these three phases is critical. Following this sequence can help increase innovation and ingenuity in your team. Phase 3 asks, "What are we doing?" Phase 4 is how will the group achieve that goal? Phase 5 focuses on the details of "who, what, when, and where"—the implementation phase. Most teams mix these three types of inquiry together, often starting with phase 5—who will do what, when, and where, skipping the how and sometimes even skipping the what (goal).

Here is an example that highlights the rigorous thinking and innovation that can occur when you do each of these three phases separately, in order, and with great intentionality. Imagine you are standing on the shore of a beach. You look out across the water and there is a lighthouse on an island. You are standing with your team and your goal is to get the entire team to the lighthouse. This is the answer to the phase 3 question— our goal is to get to the lighthouse.

The next question is, "How will we get there?" (phase 4). Here is where real creativity and process redesign can come into play. If people suspend disbelief and are allowed to be creative, they can come up with many ways to get to the island. For example, we can fly. We can take a helicopter. Ride a dolphin. Scuba dive. Build a bridge. And so many more possibilities.

One side note here, increasing your facilitation skills will dramatically improve your leadership, helping you skillfully lead activities like brainstorming, which will elicit more participation and creativity from your teams. I teach a course called "Mastering Group Facilitation." Graduates say it is a game changer. It changes how people in their organizations have conversations, improves the effectiveness of meetings, increases creativity, and more. There are many ways to encourage innovation by using different ways of talking with each other. Sometimes it is just that simple—change the way the conversation is structured. There are thousands of facilitation techniques on the web. One site I use frequently is Liberating Structures (www.liberatingstructures.com).

Let's go back to the Drexler-Sibbet model. We are still standing on the shore. We know what our purpose is. We have some innovative ways of achieving our purpose. Now we move to phase 5, which is implementation. Here is where we get to brass tacks about who will do what, when, and where. If we've decided to ride dolphins to the island, who will catch the dolphins? When? Who will train the dolphins? You get the idea.

You might notice that each of us has a preference for one of these three phases in the model. The visionary thinkers—the strategic thinkers—usually love to play in the space of phases 3 and 4. The brass tacks staff members—the engineers, the accountants—much prefer often to be in the phase 5 space. Just naming the fact that people have a preference for different types of thinking can help your team be more open to each other's different styles.

I want to make a few more points about the Drexler-Sibbet model. Note that different staff members can be at different phases, and one phase is not better than another. A 2-year-old child is not better than an 11-year-old child. A 30-year-old human being is not better than a 50-year-old human being. Each is in its own appropriate developmental space.

Teams can go back and forth between phases. When a new team member is hired, the entire team is going to go back to phases 1 and 2 because the existing team members do not know the new team member. One of the arts of using a team building model is knowing when to work with the entire team on a particular phase and when to work with various individual staff members on different phases.

The last two phases are clustered together because they are the critical moments for recognition and renewal. Phase 6 is the "wow—high performance" moment. Most people overfocus on this. Even if a team is not at high performance, it can be at good performance levels or adequate performance levels for the task at hand. Try not to overfocus on the word *high*. As a manager or leader, you want to avoid making every goal such a stretch that it is exhausting to achieve. What phase 6 points out is the need to recognize when high performance has been hit, when the team has knocked it out of the park, or even just hit the targets.

That leads to phase 7, which is renewal. I find many managers and leaders neglect this phase and run the risk of exhausting their teams both psychologically and physically. It is important to take a moment at the end of major projects, or at the end of a particular phase of the year, to renew and reflect with the team.

James Bundy, dean of the Yale University David Geffen School of Drama, used to encourage the practice of group reflection and renewal after the end of each production by bringing the entire crew together, from directors to actors to tech staff, to debrief the production. What went well? What didn't go so well? What did we learn?

He recently wrote to me to say,

> *Well, we DID do this for about the first 7–8 years but people seemed to tire of the same questions coming up. What we do now is that the managing director and I meet with every department annually to review what's gone well and what the particular challenges are. People seem to appreciate the direct discourse and it feels like we are both able to be (a) more appreciative and (b) more accountable. I do think review is important. Also, I have learned that slowing down at the beginning and in the middle also helps. Reducing the sense of urgency and reminding ourselves that people are our most important resource leads to stronger collaborations, certainly day to day, but especially when things are really hard. (email correspondence dated December 17, 2022)*

Then of course there is always celebration. Find opportunities to celebrate. Post-production party. Post-launch party. Profitable quarter lunch. A celebration can be before or after the debrief. The combination of debrief and celebration helps people ground their experience, feel appreciated, renew, and be ready to go on to the next project or task.

Here are a few more tips for team building: dedicate as much time to building your team as you do to reviewing the company's finances. If you want the "real work" to get done well and efficiently, the team has to be a high-functioning organism. To get there takes time. Every moment of every day is an opportunity to build the team if you approach it from that lens. How can the morning start build the team? How can our recruitment process build our existing team? Do we need to deepen our interpersonal connections so we better understand each other?

Be the team member you want your staff members to be. What are the competencies you ask for in them? Model those. Get feedback about how well you are doing in exhibiting those competencies. If you have not had a 360-degree feedback assessment done, consider doing so, and then do it every two years. Have your managers and leaders undertake one as well.

Let success be a reinforcing driver of teamwork. Literature and research in many fields (education, motivation, strategy) show that positive reinforcement leads to more success than negative feedback. Provide opportunities for your team, if it is a new one, to have some early wins.

For all teams, recognize success, even daily if appropriate. Work with your team to unpack the factors that led to those successes so they can tie success to specific actions. But do not be pollyannaish in this focus on success. Develop productive, non-punitive ways to take apart events and processes to see what can be improved. One rule for these unpacking sessions is to not allow the use of anyone's names. Focus on what in the system is not working or making it hard for people and the team to be successful.

Behavior: Delegates

I have covered delegation already in the book as part of the discussion on managing your time well. I covered the 4 Ds model and other tips on delegation.

Behavior: Guides and Challenges Employees So That They Develop

What greater joy is there than to see staff members grow and transform themselves into an even better version of themselves? Remember my first boss in Thailand from Chapter 1, Dan Steinbock? One of the reasons he was a great abundance boss is that he developed my skills, my organizational astuteness, and my gravitas and executive presence. He did this mostly through challenge assignments and role modeling, since there were no courses to take on the Thai-Cambodian border in the early 1980s.

There are a few key elements of a good and robust staff development program. I would venture that you know about and are using most of them already. Decades ago performance reviews were unheard of; now they are standard operating procedure in most organizations. Some performance reviews and processes are better than others. That is a topic of many other books by other authors.

Here is one unique method I use in developing employees. I ask all employees at OPG or in our client organizations to always have three résumés ready. One is a résumé for the next job in our firm or in the company in which they are working. The second résumé is for a job outside the organization in which they are working. The third résumé is for a different career or for a brand new path in their work, for example, switching from teaching to research.

What I am aiming for in asking for these three résumés is to expand the staff member's thinking about their career and what is possible for them to do in their lives. I want them to take control of their careers and realize their dreams. Most people have been taught not to share their dreams, their goals, and their hopes with their boss. At OPG we work diligently to create an atmosphere in which people can share their career plans in an open way. We want to support them in this growth, and we want the firm to be able to plan.

This three-résumés habit also decreases fear about their employment options. This in turn helps them take more risks as an organizational citizen. If people feel they have alternative employment options, they might be more willing to share ideas and critiques in their current job.

We ask employees for up to six months' or a year's notice if they are planning to go off to school, to change careers, or to change organizations. We have had great success with this attitude. Once the employee is over their fear of sharing their plans, they realize that we will not treat them any differently even if they are leaving OPG, and we are grateful for the notice and happy to support them in their journey.

Tips and Activities for Team Building

- Coordinate and empower informal teams within and across disciplines.
- Grant authority and accountability.
- Provide knowledge and then delegate.
- Celebrate team accomplishments; give the credit away.
- Help employees articulate their career paths.

COMMUNICATION

Human communication can be a hot mess that takes work to untangle and make functional. There are thousands of books, blogs, and tips on improving communication. I strongly recommend this area of study for personal and professional development. Here I will share a few communication concepts that we frequently teach or use at OPG.

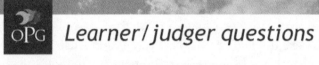

FIGURE 10.2 Learner and judger questions.

SOURCE: Adams (2022).

Tony differentiates between a learning and a judging mindset (see Figure 10.2). Although a cliché, a paradigm shift is important to create better relationships with staff members and better outcomes for your organization. A key way to do this is to develop a learning, instead of judging, mindset.

Judging, when used inappropriately, can cause people to retreat or defend their positions. When we are developing someone or working with them on a project, if we lead with negative judgment about what they are doing, with less than artful phraseology, we can risk shutting down the relationship and having them go on the defensive. Offering constructive feedback or teaching someone a new skill, or improving their skills, is *not* judging. If you have staff members who experience that type of interaction as judging, the work is then to help them see that those types of interactions are beneficial and can help them do their jobs better.

The learning mindset encourages engagement and ownership. It can also increase creativity. When you look at the questions in Figure 10.2, imagine you are on the receiving end of these questions. Notice your own reaction to the questions in each column. With which would you prefer to be approached?

You might want to put these questions up near your computer or somewhere you can see them to remind yourself to lean toward the learning mindset more often than the overly critical, judging mindset.

Another helpful concept is differentiating intention from impact, a concept developed by Tony Panos. The impact of what we say can be the opposite of what we intend, with no maliciousness or forethought. For example, I might say, "I like the red dress better on you." The impact for the listener might be that I don't like the yellow dress at all. This small transaction highlights the complexity of the communications process that begins with the construction of a thought in the sender's mind, then the sending of the thought out through words, the receiving of the thought through hearing, and finally the interpretation of the thought in the recipient's mind. Each of these steps runs risks of misunderstanding and communication breakdown, a breakdown between intention and impact.

When we get clearer about whether we are judging or trying to learn, we can get better at ensuring that our intention and impact align. This concept of intention versus impact is helpful with conflict management. Most of the time, problematic or heightened conflict arises due to poor communication. Someone says something that affects us in a negative or hurtful way. It is common for people not to check with the other person about what their intention was. We mind-read and assume what the other person intended their impact to be, instead of approaching them from a learner mindset and asking about their intention.

Behavior: Proactively Shares as Much Information as Possible

Many leaders believe that information must be meted out cautiously. Then they are surprised when staff members make bad decisions or work is not done in the way they expected. Without information, as much as possible, staff members cannot make the complex macro and micro decisions that add up to success for them, their team, and their organization.

Transparent leadership is a key Abundance Leadership behavior. This means leading with openness and honesty. These types of leaders keep their team in the loop, share information freely, and invite open communication within their departments.

Open book management is a concept that was developed a long time ago and embodies the ultimate act of transparency. Open book management means sharing the financials with staff members. That's it in its most simple manifestation. I recommend sharing as much financial information as you can. Remember that money is a form of energy that moves an organization forward. It is a game changer to provide financial education to your staff members. Teach them how to read a profit-and-loss statement, teach them how to read a balance sheet, and you will have extraordinary organizational citizens.

You do not have to share every detail of the finances but continue to push the envelope a bit. This empowers people at the front lines to understand the impact of their decisions on the financial well-being of the organization. The organizational health measure, discussed in Chapter 4, includes financial health, which I consider to be a baseline measure of organizational health similar to blood pressure or oxygen level in a person.

Behavior: Seeks Out Feedback and Receives It with Openness; Willingly Learns from Mistakes

I have addressed this in detail in the section on reflection and affect, so just a few more thoughts here on the topic. I think this is one of the hardest things to do. There are times in our lives when we just are not up for receiving feedback. Or it is not appropriate for that particular person to give us feedback or for us to give it to them. Giving and receiving feedback is based on a mutually understood psychological contract that doing so is appropriate to the relationship.

Critical feedback, criticism, and providing new information are essential to creating productive, high-performing organizations. Sometimes staff members see these types of input as negative. It can take time to teach staff members how to absorb feedback and information. The staff members at OPG struggle in their first year at OPG because they are not accustomed to the amount of feedback they receive on a daily basis. The feedback ranges from where to put the coffee cups to using the Oxford comma to a critique of a categorical analysis that they have conducted. Once staff members get past the first year, they often come to value the collaboration that this level of feedback represents.

One phrase I would encourage you to remove from your vocabulary when giving and receiving feedback is, "It is not personal." There is no such thing as "not personal" feedback. Anything someone says about you or your behavior is personal because you are a person and it is about you. The issue is that the word *personal* is used to mean "an attack on me," which can be an overreaction when the feedback is related to work performance or is providing instruction. Work performance feedback should not be an attack. It might be "personal" in the pure sense of the word, but it should never be about anything except skills and behaviors related to the work and organizational culture.

Tips and Activities for Communication

- Identify and use different communication modes.
- Collect data from your staff and constituents in a variety of ways: direct dialogue, interviews, surveys, observations.
- Ask questions and more questions: don't judge the answers.
- Use learning questions.
- Before reacting to something, check in with yourself to see if you are in learner or judger mode.
- Practice new language.
- Seek out others for their feedback and thank them for it!
- Stop emailing after two exchanges and pick up the phone or walk down the hall. Put the keyboard down.
- Take the adjectives and adverbs out of your language when describing something someone has done. Instead of "You are such a grump," try "I wanted to check in about how you are feeling. It seems to be that you might be unhappy but I wanted to hear from you. I'm checking in because your affect has an impact on me."
- Articulate your understanding of an issue or situation as a way to check if you have understood the other person's point of view.
- Instead of calling, go see the person.

PROTECTION

The competency "protection" is not found in any other leadership models of which I'm aware. Yet the feeling of protection and support is critical for staff members. It's not so much a motivating factor as a *hygiene* factor. "Frederick Herzberg theorized that employee satisfaction has two dimensions: 'hygiene' and motivation. Hygiene issues, such as salary and supervision, decrease employees' dissatisfaction with the work environment. Motivators, such as recognition and achievement, make workers more productive, creative and committed" (Syptak, Marsland, and Ulmer 1999).

When staff members feel that their leader is advocating for resources and protecting them from abusive conditions, they have, at a minimum, a safe work "container" in which to work.

Behaviors: (1) Protects Staff Members from Abusive Conditions and (2) Seeks Out Resources and Is Able to Gain Resources for Their Staff Members

These two behaviors are related. There is the reactive or defensive posture of keeping abusive conditions at bay, and there is the proactive behavior seeking out resources for your staff.

Protecting your staff from abusive conditions includes ensuring that they are not in intolerable physical workspaces or workspaces that could damage their health. Protection from abusive conditions also includes not allowing customers to yell at them or putting them in harm's way. There are many other opportunities and ways to protect your staff members from abusive conditions. One acid test might be to imagine yourself in any of your staff members' jobs. Ask yourself if you would tolerate the conditions in which they are working. The conditions might be great, and your answer is a resounding yes. But what if the answer is no?

For example, I have seen, in my consulting work, employees who are in windowless rooms in basements. For years. Would you tolerate that? Or how about an employee earning below the livable wage threshold? Or an employee who has an incompetent or abusive manager? Would you expect such an employee to be healthy and productive?

Seeking resources is the proactive side of the coin. Most of the time this is evinced in finding more funding. It can also be seen in finding more staff members, more or better physical space, better software, or advocating for your staff members' promotions.

Behavior: Maintains Healthy Organizational and Psychological Boundaries for Themselves and Their Team

One of the most powerful concepts I discovered years ago and often share with my clients is psychological contracting, which helps us keep healthy boundaries.

The psychological contract refers to the unwritten, intangible agreement between an employee and their employer that describes the informal commitments, expectations and understandings that make up their relationship.

The psychological contract shouldn't be confused with a written employment contract—they are two very separate things. An employment contract sets out the legally binding agreement between the two parties—but that contract on its own provides a very narrow and reductive view of the employee-employer relationship as a whole.

That relationship is also composed of many other expectations that, whilst not fully normalized, are just as important. While an employment contract is a legal agreement printed on paper, the psychological contract is built from the everyday actions, statements and promises of one side of the relationship and how they are received by the other.

An employment contract deals with the transactional exchange of labour for reward. The psychological contract describes the more informal perception of what each side commits to the relationship and what they might receive in return.

Aspects of a psychological contract could include any of the following:

> *Job security*
> *Opportunities for promotion*
> *Opportunities to learn and improve (Learning and Development)*
> *The employer's reputation in society*
> *The perception that the employee's work contributes positively to society*
> *A supportive manager*
> *A perception of fairness in the company's internal processes*
> *The perceived fairness of pay*
> *An expectation to go "above and beyond"*
> *The perceived fairness of a Perks and Benefits package (Enright 2022)*

At the beginning of all relationships, psychological contracts are being formed; the "contracts" are full of expectations about rights, responsibilities, behaviors, goals, and compensation in all its forms. Most aspects of these contracts are not articulated. All psychological contracts encounter problems in interpretation; this is okay and inevitable. We are, after all, talking about interactions between human beings here, the species with the most complex interpersonal signaling system on the planet. Maybe dolphins and birds come in a close second?

What matters is whether the parties to the contract have a way of talking about not only the explicit expectations but the implicit deal as well (see Figure 10.3). As an example, think about how your company

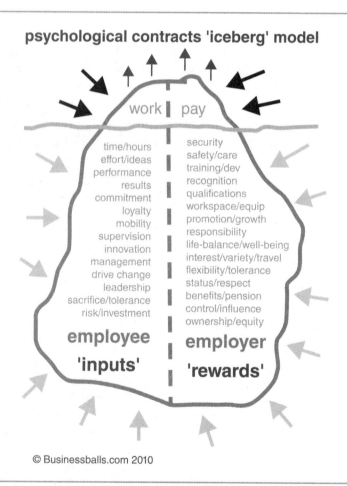

© Businessballs.com 2010

FIGURE 10.3   Most expectations are implicit.

Source: https://www.businessballs.com/collaboration-and-sharing-best-practice/the-psychological-contract. Last accessed February 20, 2023.

hires people. The position posting itself is the beginning of forming a psychological contract with that staff member. If the position posting says "innovative culture with flexible scheduling" and the person arrives to find that there is a rigid 9–5, 5-days-a-week schedule, there is likely to be a breakdown in the implicit and explicit contracts.

Here's another example of psychological contract breakdown. If a position posting does not mention the fact that your company expects everyone to share computers, the new employee will be shocked to find this to be true on their first day because the *implicit* contract with employees in this era is that each one will have their own computer.

When there is an issue in your team or organization, one question to ask is, What are our implicit and explicit contracts with each other, as boss and employee, and as organization and employee? Here, you represent the organization. Part of the art of good managing and leading is to surface the implicit psychological contract from day 1 and as it evolves.

Similar to good contracts, healthy boundaries are also critical for all relationships (Figures 10.4 and 10.5). Different types of relationships call for different boundaries. We have different boundaries with our spouses than we do with staff members. It helps increase our overall effectiveness if we are conscious of which types of boundaries we have with each person in our lives, and to change those boundaries as our needs and expectations with that person change.

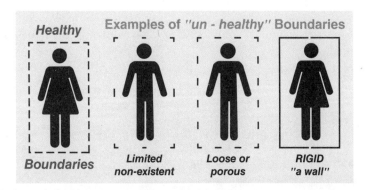

FIGURE 10.4   Types of personal boundaries.

SOURCE: https://sharingmysong.com. Last accessed February 15, 2023.

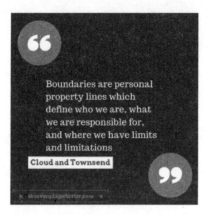

Boundaries are personal property lines which define who we are, what we are responsible for, and where we have limits and limitations

Cloud and Townsend

FIGURE 10.5   Personal property lines.

SOURCE: Cloud and Townsend.

Boundaries are manifested in many ways, including in interactions concerning these issues:

- What is disclosed to a person; what is withheld
- How and when feedback is given
- Physical touching
- Giving or receiving orders
- Expectations of assistance in different situations

Here are some questions to help you with boundaries and contracting:

- Are your rights and responsibilities clear and appropriate for this relationship?
- Are the boundaries clear and well maintained?
- Are either of you overstepping boundaries in an inappropriate way?

Tips and Activities for Protection

- Discover nonbudget resources that can assist your people to accomplish their work.
- Identify, encourage, and challenge ways for people to live a more balanced life.

> ➤ Become an active advocate of your people.
> ➤ Hire slowly; terminate quickly.
> ➤ Be mindful of your assumptions. If an assumption is in play, get more data. See if the assumption is positive or negative.
> ➤ Check for the other person's understanding of the psychological contract between the two of you.
> ➤ Remember that contracting is a two-way street. You are just as entitled as the other person to have your needs met.

DECISION-MAKING

A leader of a nonprofit gathers her staff members and asks them their opinion on which copier to buy. There is a long discussion of the pros and cons of different functions of a copier, pricing, and other factors related to the decision. A consultant is standing outside the door to the meeting room and, as staff members leave, the consultant asks each of them if it was time well spent. Each staff member says, "No, this was not time well spent. The executive director could have made the decision on her own."

Abundance leaders, like all good leaders, adapt their decision-making style to the problem and context, and don't waste their own or their staff members' time using the wrong decision-making method for the issue at hand. Let's explore some ways to become a better decision-maker.

Behaviors: (1) Is Decisive and (2) Does Not Make Inappropriately Dictatorial Decisions

Fake or overused consensus in decision-making is one of the most frequent decision-making mistakes leaders make. Leaders in the United States often default to seeking consensus, seeing it as the holy grail of group decision-making, believing that this is either the only or at least a good way to ensure buy-in to the decision and to seem inclusive. There are several problems with this choice of decision-making style, including but not limited to the following:

> ➤ First and foremost, most decisions should not be made by consensus. Victor Vroom's research shows that 60% to 80% of situationally appropriate decision-making styles ultimately rely on the leader having the final say.

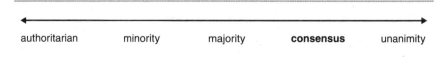

FIGURE 10.6   Spectrum of decision-making types.
SOURCE: OPG/Laura Freebairn-Smith.

> Fake consensus is when the leader pretends the decision is being made by consensus, but it isn't, which creates significant skepticism, distrust, and disengagement.
> Consensus can result in poor decisions with bad outcomes if individual experts' input is not honored; this is sometimes known as "groupthink."

Let's look at why consensus should not be the default for group decision-making. I'll review two models: (1) the spectrum of group engagement and (2) Victor Vroom's Situational Leadership model.

Spectrum of Group Engagement

There are many ways that groups make decisions, with consensus being only one of them. The styles on the spectrum, moving left to right, increase the number of people included in the process, and usually lengthen the time needed to make the decision (Figure 10.6).

Each of these methods has pros and cons. A sample of each is provided in Table 10.1.

Here are some additional notes about the different decision-making or inclusion methods to keep in mind:

> People confuse unanimity and consensus.
> Unanimity exists when everyone loves the decision; try this with seemingly simple decisions like going on vacation to Hawaii or eating vanilla ice cream; you can't get unanimity with even these seemingly universally appealing choices.
> Consensus is reached when everyone feels heard, can live with the decision, and will support it outside the room. Note this last phrase. Will people support it in the hallways and kitchen?
> Avoid voting as much as possible in organizational life; it's divisive. There are ways to get a sense of direction that don't involve voting, for example, dot voting with multiple dots per person.

TABLE 10.1 Spectrum of Inclusion in Group Decision-Making

	Authoritarian	Minority	Majority	Consensus	Unanimity
Description	One person makes the decision	A small, sometimes representative, group makes the decision	There is a vote and a majority prevails	All affected parties, or representatives of affected parties, engage in the decision-making process and can live with the decision	Everyone weighs in and is thrilled with the decision
Pros	Fast	Fast	Speed depends on timeline for the vote	Slower	Slowest
	Honors expertise	Brings in more expertise	Depending on voting structure, can give a better sense of fairness	Can increase buy-in	
		Brings in more representation			
Cons	Dangerous if the decision-maker is not knowledgeable	Greater community can feel misrepresented by the minority (small) group	Easy to have a disenfranchised large minority (think of 49/51 vote results)	Overused	Unattainable
				Hard to determine if consensus has been reached	

SOURCE: Adapted from Freebairn-Smith, 2009.

Victor Vroom's Situational Leadership Model

The second model I want to introduce to you is the work of Victor Vroom, professor emeritus at the Yale School of Management. Vroom's decades of research, based on true cases and used with more than 200,000 managers worldwide, produced a taxonomy of ways leaders make decisions with their core team. Leaders who adjust their decision-making process to the situation are referred to as situational leaders. These leaders adjust their decision-making process to increase the development level of their staff members, "as defined by competence, commitment, confidence, and motivation to perform a particular task without supervision" (Vroom 2015).

Abundance leaders are able to use situational leadership adroitly. A situational leader is one who can adopt different leadership styles depending on the situation. Vroom's research shows that there are four concepts that powerful situational leaders understand and use:

- Taxonomy of leadership styles
- Effectiveness criteria
- Situational factors
- Time- and development-driven models

Vroom distinguishes five degrees of involvement of your group and team members in the decision: decide, consult individually, consult group, facilitate, and delegate (Figure 10.7).

The choice of decision-making method is assessed against four criteria: (1) the quality of the decision made, (2) the effectiveness with which the decision is implemented, (3) the amount of time consumed in making the decision, and (4) the extent to which the decision process contributes to the development of team members.

In some situations, a more autocratic or decisive approach is likely to be most effective. In others, various degrees of involvement on the part of your group or team are likely to produce better results. Being an effective leader requires recognizing when to use each of these ways of making decisions. The optimum style for a given decision will be affected by the priorities that you place on short-term considerations (e.g., minimizing time) or on those which are longer term (developing your team).

Vroom's model suggests 11 factors that a leader should consider when choosing which decision-making method to use (Vroom 2015):

- Decision significance
- Importance of commitment

Leadership Styles

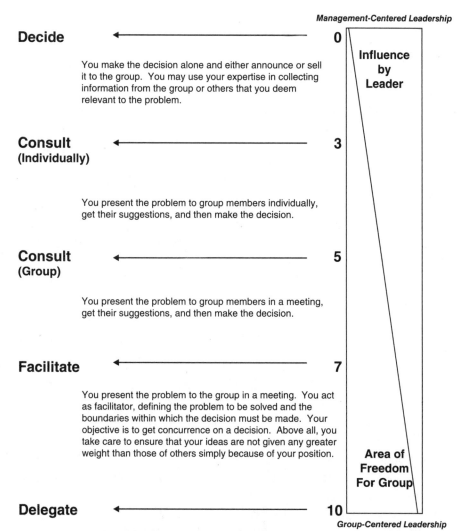

Management-Centered Leadership

Decide ⟵——————————— 0

You make the decision alone and either announce or sell it to the group. You may use your expertise in collecting information from the group or others that you deem relevant to the problem.

Influence by Leader

Consult (Individually) ⟵——————————— 3

You present the problem to group members individually, get their suggestions, and then make the decision.

Consult (Group) ⟵——————————— 5

You present the problem to group members in a meeting, get their suggestions, and then make the decision.

Facilitate ⟵——————————— 7

You present the problem to the group in a meeting. You act as facilitator, defining the problem to be solved and the boundaries within which the decision must be made. Your objective is to get concurrence on a decision. Above all, you take care to ensure that your ideas are not given any greater weight than those of others simply because of your position.

Area of Freedom For Group

Delegate ⟵——————————— 10

Group-Centered Leadership

You permit the group to make the decision within prescribed limits. The group undertakes the identification and diagnosis of the problem, developing alternative procedures for solving it, and deciding on one or more alternative solutions.

FIGURE 10.7 Vroom's decision-making methods.

SOURCE: Adapted with permission from R. Tannenbaum and W. Schmidt, "How to Choose a Leadership Pattern," *Harvard Business Review* (March–April 1958): 95–101.

- Leader's expertise
- Likelihood of commitment
- Goal alignment
- Likelihood of disagreement
- Group expertise
- Team competence
- Interaction constraint
- Importance of time
- Importance of development

David Berg, professor at Yale University, points out that there are limitations to Vroom's model. "Vroom's variable, 'likelihood of disagreement,' pushes [a leader] toward the autocratic end. This is (a) not a developmental view since we know that all well-functioning groups experience conflict, and (b) hard to square with an understanding of and commitment to real diversity (since diversity does and should lead to disagreement and conflict)" (personal communication, David Berg, December 2022).

Tips and Activities for Decision-Making

- Be transparent about which decision-making process you are going to use. If you change the process mid-decision, let your staff members know that you have done so and why.
- It's okay to make incorrect decisions but call them that and move on.
- Observe yourself and notice how you to tend to make decisions; try to use different decision-making methods suited to the situation.
- Explore what stops you from using a wider range of styles.
- Take a Vroom course, which involves a detailed assessment of your decision-making style.
- Ask others in your leadership team to do more leading and facilitating of meetings and decisions.
- Use a variety of facilitation and discussion techniques. See ideas at liberatingstructures.com.

Epilogue

I wish you the best in your journey as a leader, not an easy journey for anyone. Be kind to yourself. As I mentioned in the book, we are only perfect twice in life – at birth and death. Don't rush to perfection.

APPENDIX A

Additional Resources

Here are some additional resources to explore, some of which are mentioned in the book:

- Omega Institute (www.eomega.org): for reflection and learning
- Kripalu (www.kripalu.org): for reflection and learning
- Center for Creative Leadership (www.ccl.org): for a robust set of leadership development tools and resources
- Liberating Structures (www.liberatingstructures.org): for innovative ways to engage people in dialogue and problem solving
- Aspen Institute (www.aspeninstitute.org): for deep dialogue about a range of issues affecting the world and leaders
- Taos Institute (www.taosinstitute.net): for systems thinking about a wide range of social and other issues
- "OPG Inspire Podcast" (https://organizationalperformancegroup.com/resources/opg-inspire/)

Organizational Development Bibliography

CONSULTING

Block, Peter. *Flawless Consulting*. Wiley, 2011.

Consultants 500 Team. "Top 20 of Best Consulting Books Recommended Most Times." Consultants 500. Retrieved Feb. 16, 2021, from https://www.blog.consultants500.com/consulting/top-20-best-consulting-books-recommended-times.

Minto, Barbara. *The Pyramid Principle: Logic in Writing and Thinking*. Financial Times Prentice-Hall, 2009.

Schein, Edgar H. *Process Consultation*. Pearson Custom Publishing, 2000.

Turne, Arthur N. "Consulting Is More Than Giving Advice." *Harvard Business Review* (1982). https://hbr.org/1982/09/consulting-is-more-than-giving-advice.

DIVERSITY AND GENDER

Baker Miller, Jean. *Toward a New Psychology of Women*. Beacon Press, 1987.

Gilligan, Carol. *In a Different Voice*. Harvard University Press, 1982. I encourage you to read her most recent writings as well.

Rosener, Judy B. "Ways Women Lead." *Harvard Business Review* (1990).

Tannen, Deborah. *Talking 9–5*. Simon & Schuster, 1994. I encourage you to read any of her books as well.

Wilson, Marie C. "Introduction." *Closing the Leadership Gap: Why Women Can and Must Help Run the World*. Viking, 2004.

EVOLUTIONARY BIOLOGY

Boehm, Christopher. *Hierarchy in the Forest*. Harvard University Press, 1999. I encourage you to read any chapters of interest to you; it's a fantastic book on evolutionary biology.

Dawkins, Richard. *The Selfish Gene*, 2nd ed. Oxford University Press, 1990.

GENERAL ORGANIZATIONAL DEVELOPMENT

Ashforth, Blake. "Petty Tyranny in Organizations." *Human Relations* 47, no.7 (1994): 755–78. https://doi.org/10.1177/001872679404700701.

Bowditch, James L., and Anthony F. Buono. *A Primer on Organizational Behavior*. John Wiley & Sons, 1994.

Cha, Sandra E., and Amy C. Edmondson. "When Values Backfire: Leadership, Attribution, and Disenchantment in a Values-Driven Organization." *The Leadership Quarterly* 17, no. 1, (2006): 17, 57–78. https://doi.org/10.1016/j.leaqua.2005.10.006.

Galbraith, Jay R. *Organizational Design*. Addison-Wesley, 1977.

Ott, J. Steven. *Classic Readings in Organizational Behavior*. Brooks/Cole, 1989.

Pettigrew, Andrew M. "On Studying Organizational Cultures." *Qualitative Methodology* 24, no. 4 (1979): 570–81. https://doi.org/10.2307/2392363.

Schein, Edgar H. *Organizational Psychology*. Prentice-Hall, 1970.

LEADERSHIP

Ashforth, Blake. "Petty Tyranny in Organizations." *Human Relations* 47, no.7 (1994): 755–78. https://doi.org/10.1177/001872679404700701.

Block, Peter. "Part I: Trading Your Kingdom for a Horse." *Stewardship*. Berrett-Koehler, 1983, pp. 1–52. I encourage you to read past the chapters of Part I if you have the time.

Boehm, Christopher. *Hierarchy in the Forest*. Harvard University Press, 1999. I encourage you to read any chapters of interest to you; it's a fantastic book on evolutionary biology.

Bolman, Lee G., and Terrence E. Deal. *Leading with Soul: An Uncommon Journey of Spirit*. Jossey-Bass, 1995.

Bryman, Alan. "Qualitative Research on Leadership: A Critical but Appreciative Review." *Leadership Quarterly* 15, no. 6 (2004): 729–69. https://doi.org/10.1016/j.leaqua.2004.09.007.

Burns, James M. G. *Leadership*. Harper & Row, 1978. I recommend reading the Prologue and Chapters 1–2, 15–16.

Cha, Sandra E., and Amy C. Edmondson. "When Values Backfire: Leadership, Attribution, and Disenchantment in a Values-Driven Organization." *The Leadership Quarterly* 17, no. 1 (2006): 17, 57–78. https://doi.org/10.1016/j.leaqua.2005.10.006.

Chang, Edward C. *Optimism & Pessimism: Implications for Theory, Research, and Practice*. American Psychological Association, 2001.

Collins, James C. *Good to Great: Why Some Companies Make the Leap . . . and Others Don't*. HarperBusiness, 2001.

Covey, Stephen R. "Family of Ethics: You Can Start Your Own Family of Ethics." *Executive Excellence* 16, no. 8 (1999): 3.

Covey, Stephen R. *The 7 Habits of Highly Effective People: Powerful Lessons in Personal Change*. Simon & Schuster, 2013.

Daw, Kurt. Chapter 2. Unpublished Dissertation.

Dinkmeyer, Don, and Lewis Losoncy. *The Skills of Encouragement: How to Bring Out the Best in Yourself and Others*. St. Lucie, 1996.

Ekvall, Göran, and Jouko Arvonen. "Change-Centered Leadership: An Extension of the Two-Dimensional Model." *Scandinavian Journal of Management* 7, no. 1 (1991): 17–26. https://doi.org/10.1016/0956-5221(91)90024-U.

Goleman, Daniel. "What Makes a Leader?" *Harvard Business Review* (Nov.-Dec., 1998): 93–102.

Gronn, Peter. "Substituting for Leadership: The Neglected Role of the Leadership Couple." *The Leadership Quarterly* 10, no. 1 (1999): 41–62. https://doi.org/10.1016/S1048-9843(99)80008-3.

Machiavelli, Niccolò. *The Prince*. Penguin Books, 1981. I recommend you read Chapters XVIII, XXI–XXIII.

Mindwalk. Directed by Fritjof Capra, Atlas Production Company, 1990.

Pearce, Craig L., and Henry P. Sims. "Vertical Versus Shared Leadership as Predictors of the Effectiveness of Change Management Teams: An Examination of Aversive, Directive, Transactional, Transformational, and Empowering Leader Behaviors." *Group Dynamics: Theory, Research, and Practice* 6, no. 2 (2002): 172–97. https://doi.org/10.1037/1089-2699.6.2.172.

Pepper, John. *What Really Matters: Service, Leadership, People, and Values*. Yale University Press, 2007.

Podsakoff, Philip M., Scott B. MacKenzie, Robert H. Moorman, and Richard Fetter. "Transformational Leader Behaviors and Their Effects on Followers' Trust in Leader, Satisfaction, and Organizational Citizenship Behaviors." *The Leadership Quarterly* 1, no. 2 (1990): 107–42.

Rosener, Judy B. "Ways Women Lead." *Harvard Business Review* (1990).

Sternberg, Robert J., and Victor Vroom. "The Person Versus the Situation in Leadership." *The Leadership Quarterly* 13, no. 3(2002): 301–23. https://doi.org/10.1016/S1048–9843(02)00101–7.

Suzuki, Shunryū, and Trudy Dixon. *Zen Mind, Beginner's Mind*. Shambhala, 2010.

Vroom, Victor H., and Philip W. Yetton. *Leadership and Decision-Making*. University of Pittsburgh Press, 2017.

Wheatley, Margaret J. *Leadership and the New Science: Discovering Order in a Chaotic World*. Berrett-Koehler, 2018.

Wielkiewicz, Richard M., and Stephen P. Stelzner. "An Ecological Perspective on Leadership Theory, Research, and Practice." *Review of General Psychology* 9, no.4 (2005): 326–41. https://doi.org/10.1037/1089–2680.9.4.326.

Wilson, Marie C. "Introduction." *Closing the Leadership Gap: Why Women Can and Must Help Run the World*. Viking, 2004.

MANAGING CHANGE

Beckhard, Richard, and Reuben T. Harris. *Organizational Transitions: Managing Complex Change*. Addison-Wesley, 1977.

Ertel, Chris, and Lisa K. Solomon. *Moments of Impact: How to Design Strategic Conversations That Accelerate Change*. Simon & Schuster, 2014.

MISCELLANEOUS

Adams, J. *The Meaning of Wealth*. Unpublished manuscript (2004).

Boldt, Laurence G. *The Tao of Abundance: Eight Ancient Principles for Abundant Living*. Penguin Compass, 1999.

Bookchin, Murray. *Post-Scarcity Anarchism*. Black Rose Books, 1971.

Creswell, John W. *Research Design: Qualitative, Quantitative, and Mixed Method Approaches*. SAGE, 2003.

Dyer, William. (2009). "Having It All." https://spiritlibrary.com/wayne-w-dyer/having-it-all.

Finnin, William M., and Gerald A. Smith. *The Morality of Scarcity: Limited Resources and Social Policy*. Louisiana State University Press, 1979.

Fricker, Alan. "Beyond Scarcity and Greed." *Futures* 30, no. 6 (1998): 559–67. https://planet.uwc.ac.za/nisl/Gwen's%20Files/Biodiversity/Chapters/Info%20to%20use/footprintNewZealandFricker.pdf.

Hawken, Paul. *The Ecology of Commerce: How Business Can Save the Planet*. Weidenfeld and Nicolson, 1993.

Heath, R. *Shadows Round the Moon*. Collins, 1990.

Marx, Karl, et al. *The Marx-Engels Reader*. Norton, 1972.

Suzuki, Shunryū, and Trudy Dixon. *Zen Mind, Beginner's Mind*. Shambhala, 2010.

Uhlein, Gabriele, and Saint Hildegard. *Meditations with Hildegard of Bingen*. Bear & Co., 1984.

POETRY

Piercy, Marge. "To Be of Use." *Cries of the Spirit*, Beacon Press, 1991, p. 172.

PSYCHOLOGY OF THE INDIVIDUAL

Carriker, Robert M., and Mary Farmer-Kaiser. *Optimism, Struggle, and Growth: Readings on an Expanding America*. Kendall/Hunt, 2001.

Chang, Edward C. *Optimism & Pessimism: Implications for Theory, Research, and Practice*. American Psychological Association, 2001.

Covey, Stephen R. *The 7 Habits of Highly Effective People: Powerful Lessons in Personal Change*. Simon & Schuster, 2013.

Keeble, J.B.I. "Scarcity vs. Abundance: Financial Planning Is Based on the 'Abundance Mentality'—The Ideal That We Can Create Enough for All." Lexis Nexis, 2001.

Maslow, Abraham H. *Toward a Psychology of Being*. Van Nostrand Reinhold, 1968.

McCrae, Robert R., and Fritz Ostendorf. "Nature Over Nurture: Temperament, Personality, and Life Span Development." *Journal of Personality and Social Psychology* 78, no. 1 (2000): 173–86. https://doi.apa.org/doi/10.1037/0022–3514.78.1.173.

Perry, J. Mitchell, and Rick Griggs. *The Road to Optimism: Change Your Language, Change Your Life*. Manfit Press, 1997.

Rossatto, Cesar A. *Engaging Paulo Freire's Pedagogy of Possibility: From Blind to Transformative Optimism*. Rowman & Littlefield, 2005.

Scheier, Michael F., Charles S. Carver, and Michael W. Bridges. "Optimism, Pessimism, and Psychological Well-Being." *Optimism and Pessimism: Implications for Theory, Research, and Practice*, ed. E. C. Chang. American Psychological Association, 2001, pp. 189–216.

Seligman, Martin E. P. *Learned Optimism: How to Change Your Mind and Your Life*. Nicholas Brealey, 2018.

Vaughan, Susan C. *Half Empty, Half Full: Understanding the Psychological Roots of Optimism*. Harcourt, 2001.

STATISTICS, DATA, AND ANALYSIS

Creswell, John W. *Research Design: Qualitative, Quantitative, and Mixed Methods Approaches*. SAGE, 2003.

Neter, John, and William Wasserman. *Applied Linear Statistical Models: Regression, Analysis of Variance, and Experimental Designs*. Richard D. Irwin, 1974.

Rosenthal, Robert, and Ralph L. Rosnow. *Essentials of Behavioral Research: Methods and Data Analysis*. McGraw-Hill, 1991.

Thurstone, L. L. *Multiple-Factor Analysis: A Development and Expansion of the Vectors of Mind*. University of Chicago Press, 1969.

STRATEGIC PLANNING

Cascade Team. "Strategy Books: Essential Strategic Reading." Cascade (Jan. 1, 2020). https://www.cascade.app/blog/strategy-books.

Collins, James C. *Good to Great: Why Some Companies Make the Leap . . . and Others Don't*. HarperBusiness, 2001.Martin, Roger L. "The Big Lie of Strategic Planning." *Harvard Business Review* 92 (2014): 79–84. https://hbr.org/2014/01/the-big-lie-of-strategic-planning.

Mintzberg, Henry. *Rise and Fall of Strategic Planning: Reconceiving Roles for Planning, Plans, Planners*. Free Press, 1994.

Dixit, Avinash K., and Barry J. Nalebuff. *A Game Theorist's Guide to Success in Business and Life*. W. W. Norton & Co., 2008.

Porter, Michael. *Competitive Strategy: Techniques for Analyzing Industries and Competitors*. Free Press, 1980.

Thompson, Gregory C., Harish Maringanti, Rick Anderson, Catherine B. Soehner, and Alberta Comer. *Strategic Planning for Academic Libraries: A Step-by-Step Guide*. ALA Editions, 2019.

SYSTEMS THINKING

Adams, John D. *Thinking Today as if Tomorrow Mattered: The Rise of a Sustainable Consciousness*. Eartheart, 2000.

Boldt, Laurence G. "The Tao of Abundance." Soulful Living (1999). Retrieved from http://www.soulfulliving.com/tao_of_abundance.htm.

Carriker, Robert M., and Mary Farmer-Kaiser. *Optimism, Struggle, and Growth: Readings on an Expanding America*. Kendall/Hunt, 2001.

Carson, Rachel. *Silent Spring*. Houghton Mifflin, 1962.

Feyerabend, Paul, and Bert Terpstra. *Conquest of Abundance: A Tale of Abstraction Versus the Richness of Being*. University of Chicago Press, 1999.

Gunderson, Lance H., and C. S. Holling. *Panarchy: Understanding Transformations in Human and Natural Systems*. Island Press, 2001.

Malthus, Thomas Robert, and Geoffrey Gilbert. *An Essay on the Principle of Population*. Oxford University Press, 2008.

Marx, Karl, et al. *The Marx-Engels Reader*. Norton, 1972.

Meadows, Donella. *Thinking in Systems*. Chelsea Green Publishing, 2008.

Mindwalk. Directed by Fritjof Capra. Atlas Production Company, 1990.

Ray, Paul. "The Rise of Integral Culture." *Noetic Sciences Review* 37, no. 4 (1996).

Senge, Peter. *The Fifth Discipline: The Art & Practice of the Learning Organization*. Currency Doubleday, 1990.

Suzuki, Shunryū, and Trudy Dixon. *Zen Mind, Beginner's Mind*. Shambhala, 2010.

Wheatley, Margaret J. *Leadership and the New Science: Discovering Order in a Chaotic World*. Berrett-Koehler, 2018.

Wielkiewicz, Richard M., and Stephen P. Stelzner. "An Ecological Perspective on Leadership Theory, Research, and Practice." *Review of General Psychology* 9, no. 4 (2005): 326–41. https://doi.org/10.1037/1089–2680.9.4.326.

TEAM BUILDING AND GROUP FACILITATION

Beckhard, Richard, and Reuben T. Harris. *Organizational Transitions: Managing Complex Change*. Addison-Wesley, 1977.

Bowditch, James L., and Anthony F. Buono. *A Primer on Organizational Behavior*. John Wiley & Sons, 1994.

Cain, Susan. *Quiet: The Power of Introverts in a World That Won't Stop Talking*. Crown, 2013.

Dinkmeyer, Don, and Lewis Losoncy. *The Skills of Encouragement: How to Bring Out the Best in Yourself and Others*. St. Lucie, 1996.

Dyer, William G. *Team Building: Issues and Alternatives*. Addison-Wesley, 1987.

Galbraith, Jay R. *Organizational Design*. Addison-Wesley, 1977.

Gillette, Jonathon, and Marion McCollom. *Groups in Context: A New Perspective on Group Dynamics*. University Press of America, 1995.

Hackman, J. Richard. *Groups That Work (and Those That Don't): Creating Conditions for Effective Teamwork*. Jossey-Bass, 1991.

Johnson-Laird, Philip N. *Mental Models: Towards a Cognitive Science of Language, Inference, and Consciousness*. Harvard University Press, 1983.

Lipmanowicz, Henri, and Keith McCandless. *The Surprising Power of Liberating Structures*. Liberating Structures Press, 2014.

Mathieu, J. E., T. S. Heffner, G. F. Goodwin, E. Salas, and J. A. Cannon-Bowers. (2000). "The Influence of Shared Mental Models on Team Process and Performance." *Journal of Applied Psychology* 85, no. 2 (2000): 273–283. https://doi.org/10.1037/0021–9010.85.2.273.

Ott, J. Steven. *Classic Readings in Organizational Behavior*. Brooks/Cole, 1989.

Parker, Priya. *The Art of Gathering: How We Meet and Why It Matters*. Riverhead Books, 2020.

Reddy, W. Brendan, and Kaleel Jamison. *Team Building: Blueprints for Productivity and Satisfaction*. NTL Institute for Applied Behavioral Science, 1988.

Rouse, W. B., and N. M. Morris. "On Looking into the Black Box: Prospects and Limits in the Search for Mental Models." *Psychological Bulletin* 100, no. 3 (1986): 349–363. https://doi.org/10.1037/0033–2909.100.3.349.

Schein, Edgar H. *Organizational Psychology*. Prentice-Hall, 1970.

Smith, Kenwyn K., and David N. Berg. *Paradoxes of Group Life: Understanding Conflict, Paralysis, and Movement in Group Dynamics*. Jossey-Bass, 1997.

Vroom, Victor H., and Philip W. Yetton. *Leadership and Decision-Making*. University of Pittsburgh Press, 2017.

Weisbrod, Marvin R. *Productive Workplaces*. Jossey-Bass, 1987.

References

Adams, John D. *Thinking Today as if Tomorrow Mattered: The Rise of a Sustainable Consciousness*. Eartheart, 2000.

Adams, John D. *The Meaning of Wealth*. Unpublished manuscript (2004).

Adams, Marilee. *Change Your Questions, Change Your Life: 12 Powerful Tools for Leadership, Coaching, and Results*, 4th ed. Berrett-Koehler Publishers, 2022.

Arayandas, Das, Joshua D. Margolis, and Ryan Raffaelli. "Ron Johnson: A Career in Retail." Harvard Business School Case 516–016 (July 2015).

Bolman, Lee G., and Terrence E. Deal. *Leading with Soul: An Uncommon Journey of Spirit*. Jossey-Bass, 1995.

Bookchin, Murray. *Post-Scarcity Anarchism*. Black Rose Books, 1971.

Brumberg, Rovvy. "How Communicators Can Bolster Workplace Emotional Intelligence." *Ragan Insider* (2019). https://www.ragan.com/how-communicators-can-bolster-workplace-emotional-intelligence/.

Bryman, Alan. "Qualitative Research on Leadership: A Critical but Appreciative Review." *Leadership Quarterly* 15, no. 6 (2004): 729–69. https://doi.org/10.1016/j.leaqua.2004.09.007.

Buckingham, Marcus. "What Great Managers Do." *Harvard Business Review* (2005).

Bursztynsky, Jessica. "Delta Air Lines CEO Announces the Carrier Will Go 'Fully Carbon Neutral' Next Month." CNBC (Feb. 14, 2020). https://www.cnbc.com/2020/02/14/delta-air-lines-ceo-carrier-will-go-fully-carbon-neutral-next-month.html.

Caldwell, C am, and Linda A. Hayes. "Self-Efficacy and Self-Awareness: Moral Insights to Increased Leader Effectiveness." *Journal of Management Development* 35, no. 9 (2016): 1163–1173. https://doi.org/10.1108/JMD-01–2016–0011.

Carlson, Jessica H., and M. Crawford. "Perceptions of Relational Practices in the Workplace." *Gender, Work, and Organization* 18 (2011): 359–376.

Carson, Rachel. *Silent Spring*. Houghton Mifflin, 1962.

Cha, Sandra, and Amy C. Edmondson. "When Values Backfire: Leadership, Attribution, and Disenchantment in a Values-Driven Organization." *The Leadership Quarterly* 17 (2006): 57–78.

Center for Management & Organization Effectiveness. "13 of the Most Influential Leaders in Business." Retrieved November 12, 2022, from https://cmoe.com/blog/13-of-the-most-influential-leaders-in-business.

Covey, Stephen R. "Family of Ethics: You Can Start Your Own Family of Ethics." *Executive Excellence* 16, no. 8 (1999): 3.

Covey, Stephen R. *Primary Greatness: The 12 Levers of Success*. Simon & Schuster. 2015.

Daw, C. D. *"Creating a Transformational Environment in a Public Senior College"* (1996). Retrieved from https://www.proquest.com/openview/d23 734a97bd76d29948cc2ac894e9cbf/1?pq-origsite=gscholar&cbl=18750& diss=y.

Dawkins, Richard. *The Selfish Gene*, 2nd ed. Oxford University Press, 1990.

Dillard, A. *The Writing Life*. Harper Perennial, 2013.

Dinkmeyer, Don, and Lewis Losoncy. *The Skills of Encouragement: How to Bring Out the Best in Yourself and Others*. St. Lucie, 1996.

Eisenhauer, T. "Leadership Without Ego: How to Get Your Ego Out of the Way?" (n.d.).

Enright, Jack. (2022). "What Is the Psychological Contract?" Retrieved December 17, 2022, from www.charliehr.com/blog/what-is-the-psychological-contract/.

Fabrega, M. (2022). "10 Ways to Tame Your Monkey Mind and Stop Mental Chatter." Retrieved January 30, 2023, from https://daringtolivefully.com/ tame-your-monkey-mind.

Feyerabend, Paul, and Bert Terpstra. *Conquest of Abundance: A Tale of Abstraction Versus the Richness of Being*. University of Chicago Press, 1999.

Finnin, William M., and Gerald A. Smith. *The Morality of Scarcity: Limited Resources and Social Policy*. Louisiana State University Press, 1979.

Freebairn-Smith, L. *"Abundance and Scarcity Mental Models in Leaders"* (2009). https://organizationalperformancegroup.com/wp-content/uploads/ 2019/02/10.1.1.470.3812.pdf.

Fricker, Alan. "Beyond Scarcity and Greed." *Futures* 30, no. 6 (1998): 559–67. https://planet.uwc.ac.za/nisl/Gwen's%20Files/Biodiversity/Chapters/ Info%20to%20use/footprintNewZealandFricker.pdf.

Goman, Carol Kinsey. "Five Ways Body Language Impacts Leadership Results" (2018). https://www.forbes.com/sites/carolkinseygoman/2018/08/26/5-ways-body-language-impacts-leadership-results/?sh=62bc6aac536a. 2018.

Govindarajan, Vijay, and Srikantha Srinivas. "The Innovation Mindset in Action: 3M Corporation." *Harvard Business Review* (March 2013).

Gunderson, Lance H., and C. S. Holling. *Panarchy: Understanding Transformations in Human and Natural Systems*. Island Press, 2001.

Hall, Douglas T. *Self-Awareness, Identity, and Leader Development*. Psychology Press, 2004.

Hancock, L. "An Idea Whose Time Has Come: The Four-Day Workweek." *Baltimore Sun* (2021). https://www.baltimoresun.com/opinion/op-ed/bs-ed-op-0926-four-day-workweek-20210924-h57n7wvcnnhtjg5qr44j4ov2qy-story.html.

Hawken, Paul. *The Ecology of Commerce: How Business Can Save the Planet*. Weidenfeld and Nicolson, 1993.

Hlebowitsh, N. "What's the Difference Between Cognitive vs. Emotional Intelligence?" (April 22, 2021). https://thinkpsych.com/blog/cognitive-vs-emotional-intelligence/.

Hessekiel, D. "Changemaker Interview: Hamdi Ulukaya, Founder & CEO, Chobani." *Forbes*. Retrieved Sept. 28, 2022, from https://www.forbes.com/sites/davidhessekiel/2020/09/25/changemaker-interview-hamdi-ulukaya-founder—ceo-chobani/?sh=194334417a17.

Hochschild, Arlene R. *The Managed Heart: Commercialization of Human Feeling*. University of California Press, 2012.

Johnson-Laird, Philip N. *Mental Models: Towards a Cognitive Science of Language, Inference, and Consciousness*. Harvard University Press, 1983.

Keating, Steve. *"Leadership Visibility"* (2022). https://stevekeating.me/2022/05/05/leadership-visibility/.

Keeble, J.B.I. *"Scarcity vs. Abundance: Financial Planning Is Based on the 'Abundance Mentality'—The Ideal That We Can Create Enough for All."* Lexis Nexis, 2001.

Keltner, Dacher, and Jonathan Haidt. "Social Functions of Emotions at Four Levels of Analysis." *Cognition and Emotion* 13, no. 5 (1999): 505–21.

Kozol, Jonathan. *Savage Inequalities: Children in America's Schools*. New York: Crown, 1991.

Lombard, Catherine Ann. "Psychosynthesis: A Foundational Bridge Between Psychology and Spirituality." *Pastoral Psychology* 66 (2017): 461–85.

Lovering, N. "How We Use Fluid vs. Crystallized Intelligence." PsychCentral (2021). https://psychcentral.com/health/fluid-vs-crystallized-intelligence#differences.

Malthus, Thomas Robert, and Geoffrey Gilbert. *An Essay on the Principle of Population*. Oxford University Press, 2008. (Originally published in 1797.)

Manasa Showry, K. "Self-Awareness Key to Effective Leadership." *IUP Journal of Soft Skills* 8, no. 1 (2014): 15–26.

Marshall, D. *"11 Situations Where Your Organization Needs OD"* (2017). https://ideas.bkconnection.com/11-situations-where-your-organization-needs-od.

Mathieu, J. E., T. S. Heffner, G. F. Goodwin, E. Salas, and J. A. Cannon-Bowers. (2000). "The Influence of Shared Mental Models on Team Process and Performance." *Journal of Applied Psychology* 85, no. 2 (2000): 273–283. https://doi.org/10.1037/0021–9010.85.2.273.

McCrae, Robert R., and Fritz Ostendorf. "Nature Over Nurture: Temperament, Personality, and Life Span Development." *Journal of Personality and Social Psychology* 78, no. 1 (2000): 173–86. https://doi.apa.org/doi/10.1037/0022–3514.78.1.173.

McKee, Annie. "How Leaders Moods and Emotions Impact Their Companies" (Oct. 18, 2018). http://www.anniemckee.com/leaders-moods-emotions-impact-companies/.

Morgan, Blake. "*15 Of The World's Most Inspiring Female Leaders*" (2021). https://www.forbes.com/sites/blakemorgan/2021/03/07/15-of-the-worlds-most-inspiring-female-leaders/?sh=200f9d7b3e6e.

Nalebuff, Barry, and Ian Ayers. *Why Not? How to Use Everyday Ingenuity to Solve Problems Big and Small.* Harvard Business School Press, 2003.

Perry, J. Mitchell, and Rick Griggs. *The Road to Optimism: Change Your Language, Change Your Life.* Manfit Press, 1997.

Piercy, Marge. "To Be of Use." *Cries of the Spirit.* Beacon Press, 1991, p. 172.

Porter, Michael. *Competitive Strategy: Techniques for Analyzing Industries and Competitors.* Free Press, 1980.

Ray, Paul. "The Rise of Integral Culture." *Noetic Sciences Review* 37, no. 4 (1980).

Rossatto, Cesar A. *Engaging Paulo Freire's Pedagogy of Possibility: From Blind to Transformative Optimism.* Rowman & Littlefield, 2005.

Rouse, William B., and Nancy M. Morris. "On Looking into the Black Box: Prospects and Limits in the Search for Mental Models." Psychological Bulletin 100, no. 3 (1986): 349–363. https://doi.org/10.1037/0033–2909.100.3.349.

Scheier, Michael F., Charles S. Carver, and Michael W. Bridges. "Optimism, Pessimism, and Psychological Well-Being." *Optimism and Pessimism: Implications for Theory, Research, and Practice*, ed. E. C. Chang. American Psychological Association, 2001, pp. 189–216.

Seattle, Chief. "Texts by and About Natives: Texts 8. Ted Perry, "Chief Seattle's Speech." Retrieved January 30, 2023, from https://www.washington.edu/uwired/outreach/cspn/Website/Classroom%20Materials/Reading%20the%20Region/Texts%20by%20and%20about%20Natives/Texts/8.html.

Seligman, Martin E. P. *Learned Optimism: How to Change Your Mind and Your Life.* Vintage Books, 1990.

Stange, Jocelyn. 2021). "How to Deal with Emotions in the Workplace." https://www.quantumworkplace.com/future-of-work/emotions-in-the-workplace-how-to-deal-with-emotions-at-work.

Syptak, J. Michael, David W. Marsland Jr., and Deborah Ulmer. "Job Satisfaction: Putting Theory into Practice. *Family Practice Management* 6, no. 9 (1999): 26–30.

Tannenbaum, R., and W. Schmidt, "How to Choose a Leadership Pattern." *Harvard Business Review* (March–April 1958): 95–101.

Tucker, Robert C., ed. *The Marx-Engels reader*. W. W. Norton, 1972.

Uhlein, Gabriele, and Saint Hildegard. *Meditations with Hildegard of Bingen*. Bear & Co., 1984.

Vaughan, Susan C. *Half Empty, Half Full: Understanding the Psychological Roots of Optimism*. Harcourt, 2001.

Vroom, Victor H. *Decision Making for Leaders: Trainer's Manual*. Self-published (2015).

Vroom, Victor H., and Philip W. Yetton. *Leadership and Decision-Making*. University of Pittsburgh Press, 2017.

Waber, Ben, Jennifer Magnolfi, and Greg Lindsay. "Workspaces That Move People." *Harvard Business Review* (2014).

Willis, Daniel. "Are Charrettes Old School?" *Harvard Design Magazine* (2010). http://www.harvarddesignmagazine.org/issues/33/are-charrettes-old-school.

Wright, Gretchen, Robert Roche, and Laura Freebairn-Smith. "What's an Organizational Charrette and How Can It Enhance Your Business?" *HR Daily Advisor* (2019). https://hrdailyadvisor.blr.com/2019/02/22/whats-an-organizational-charrette-and-how-can-it-enhance-your-business/.

X Malcolm, and Alex Haley. *The Autobiography of Malcolm X*. New York: Penguin Books, 1973.

Acknowledgments

Tony Panos, my amazing partner at OPG, who brought Abundance Leadership to life and embodies it every day.

David Berg, my mentor, who showed me the power of organizational development to help people and make the world better.

The staff members of OPG, past and present, who every day make the world better through their efforts.

The teaching team in the Abundance Leadership Immersion Program: Tony Panos, John Egan, and Maria Freebairn-Smith, who have helped participants see themselves more clearly with greater self-acceptance, and helped them transform their organizations and the world.

Agata Gluszek, without whom the original research would never have revealed the insights it did.

Alumni of the Abundance Leadership Immersion Program, who are the seeds of change.

My friends, all of whom, past and present, have been sources of inspiration, support, and learning.

And most important, my beloved family: my children (Trent and Luke), my parents (Rod, Martha, Lee, and Janet), and my siblings (Maria and Sutton), who gave me the tools and love for this journey.

About the Author

Born in Montana on an Air Force base, **Laura Freebairn-Smith** grew up in San Francisco during the height of the anti-Vietnam, women's rights, and Civil Rights movements—all movements in which her parents were active.

After graduating from UC Berkeley with a BA in philosophy and political science, Laura headed to Thailand where she worked for four years as the education coordinator for the International Rescue Committee in two Cambodian refugee camps on the Thai-Cambodian border.

She went on to Yale to get her MBA, and to serve as chief operating officer and managing director for two nonprofits. She also founded and served as director of the Organizational Development & Learning Center at Yale.

She holds a PhD in organizational systems from Saybrook University. She has taught as a faculty member and guest lecturer at Yale, Georgetown, Central CT State University, and the University of New Haven.

Laura is currently a partner and cofounder of Organizational Performance Group (OPG), a management consulting firm that believes people and their ability to work together are critical to the success of all organizations www.orgpg.com.

Laura has been interviewed on a variety of podcasts and television broadcasts. OPG has its own podcast, *OPG Inspire*, on which you can hear Laura speaking on topics such as microlevers, Abundance Leadership, and more. Laura has won leadership and other awards from her community in Greater New Haven.

Laura has published many chapters and articles on topics ranging from leadership to income inequality. Most of those publications can be found on OPG's website under the Resources section. For more information on Laura and her work, visit www.orgpg.com.

Index

3M Corporation, innovation ability, 108–109
360-degree feedback, 67–68

A

Abundance, 30, 36
  behaviors, 31–32, 43, 99
      113, 145, 177
  generation, 37
  mentality, 32, 37, 101
      definition, 31–32
  mental model, 21, 25
  mirroring, 30
  model, 65
  orientation, 21–23
Abundance leaders
  objectives, adaption/application,
      41
  thinking process, 19
Abundance Leadership (AL),
      1, 63, 141
  advanced skill, 11
  behavior, 155
  competencies, 44t–45t, 96t–97t
  informing, fields (impact), 30–42
  journey, 3
  model, 3, 7
      articulation, 16
      development, 30–31
  Program, 113–114
  result, 87
  seeds, 14–15
Abundance Leadership Immersion
      Program, 8, 19, 67–68, 136
Abundance-scarcity spectrum, 24
Actions, patching/layering, 48–49
Active listening, 136

Adams, John, 41
Adaptability, 58
Adversity, confrontation, 25
Affect. *See* Reflection/affect
Anger
  feeling, rationality, 101
  power, 125
Annual donation, usage, 89–90
Anti-CEO playbook, 49–50
Aquarium (OPG conference room).
      See Organizational
      Performance Group
Ardern, Jacinda, 53–54, 54f
Aspen Institute, 169
Assertiveness, 135
Astarita, Tammy, 82
Awin, 75

B

Barber, Rob, 113–114
Bastian, Ed, 51, 51f
Behavior
  explorations, 58
  patterns, polarization, 41
Being, focus, 23
Ben & Jerry's, vision statement,
      100
Berg, David, 110, 168
Blame (scarcity behavior) (scarcity
      signal behavior), 46, 47
Body language, importance, 124
Bosses, impact, 65
Bottleneck, 138
Boundaries
  differences, 161
  manifestation/questions, 162
  setting, 129

Buddhism, 131
Buffett, Warren, 54–56, 55f
Bullying, 142
Bundy, James, 150
Burger shack, service photo, 4f
Burnout, reduction, 74
Business, promise, 40
Business Unit Laboratories, market focus, 109

C

Calendar, visibility, 115
Camaraderie, sense, 66
Cambodian refugee, 9f
Carson, Rachel, 36
Cashman, Kevin, 19
Cattiness/pettiness, presence, 66
Celebration, search, 151
Center for Creative Leadership, 169
Character-based orientation, 24
Characterological default setting, 146
Charrettes, 69–73
  defining, 70
  prep instructions, 71f
  results, 73
  usage, 70–73
Chodron, Pema, 124
Circadian-friendly work environment, creation (guidelines), 81–82
Circadian rhythm, 69
  analysis, 81f
  monthly analysis, 82f
  usage, 77–85
Clients, coaching, 101–102
  questions, usage, 122
Coaching (scarcity behavior), 45
Cognitive intelligence, 110–111
Collaboration, questions, 72
Collaborative environment, creation, 60
Collective competition, 89–90
Collective memory, 90–91
Comfort/discomfort, identification, 122

Commerce, transformation, 40
Commitment, importance/likelihood, 166
Communication, 153–157
  advice/activities, 156–157
  breakdown, 155
  control (scarcity behavior) (scarcity signal behavior), 45, 47
  effectiveness, 66
  management skills, 61
  methods, 56
  patterns, 47
Community wall, 90
Company (internal processes), fairness (perception), 159
Comparative mind, 131, 133–135
Compassion, demonstration, 136
Compensation
  impact, 118
  solving, 48–49
Competencies, 43, 99, 113, 117, 145
  exhibition, 151
  learning, 58
Condescension (scarcity behavior) (scarcity signal behavior), 46, 47
Confidence, improvement, 133
Conflict
  addressing, 136–139
  avoidance, scarcity behavior, 45
  management, 59, 155
  navigation, 137
  resolution, 66
Consensus
  impact, 163
  reaching, 164
Contact, discouragement (scarcity behavior) (scarcity signal behavior), 45, 47
Contentment, spiritual beliefs (impact), 102
Content skills, 119f
Contracting, questions, 162

Control
abdication, 130
absence, 132
Core values, sense, 122
Cossman, E. Joseph, 43
Covey, Stephen, 31–32
COVID, impact, 73–74, 77
Creativity, 107–111
advice/activities, 111
criteria, 107
encouragement, 23
encouragement (3M), 108–109
impact, 148–149
importance, 67
levels, elevation, 70
Criticism, 137
minimization, 23
Crystalized intelligence, fluid
    intelligence (contrast),
    111t
Cultural apparatus, 37
"Cultural Creatives," 42

D

Dawkins, Richard, 42
Decision-making, 162–168
advice/activities, 168
behaviors, 163–168
choice, 166
consensus, 163
group decision-making, inclusion
    (spectrum), 165t
management skill, 62
methods, 164
methods (Vroom), 167f
process, 168
    adjustment, 164
styles, 163
timeliness, 66
types, spectrum, 164f
Decision significance, 166
Defeat, temporariness, 26
Defensiveness, feeling (rationality),
    101

Delegation, 151
job functions, delegation, 102
Design professionals, engagement, 76
Development-driven models, 166
Development, importance, 166
Dewey, John, 121
Dictatorial decisions (scarcity
    behavior), 46, 163–168
Dillard, Annie, 118
Disagreements
escalation (scarcity behavior), 45
likelihood, 166
Disciplines (purity), maintenance
    (incentives), 39
Dis-ease, signs, 146
Do, Delegate, Delay, Drop (4 Ds),
    128, 135, 151
Douthwaite, Richard, 38
Drexler-Sibbet team performance
    model, 147–149, 148f
Drucker, Peter F., 19
Dual-career ladder (3M structure/
    system), 109

E

Earth, resources (limitations), 35–36
Ecology of Commerce, The
    (Hawken), 39
Ecology, theories, 39
Economic assets, access
    (improvement), 52
Economics, meaning, 38
Economic transaction, 38
Ecosystems, restoration, 41, 56
Edison, Thomas, 95
Egocentrism (scarcity behavior), 46
Ego control, 141–143
advice/activities, 143
Ego, importance, 142
Einstein, Albert, 42
Eltel, Marla, 52, 53f
Emerson, Ralph Waldo, 65
Emotional intelligence, elements,
    123f

Emotional reactions, scarcity-abundance continuum (proposed ends), 25t
Emotions
  display, impact, 126
  expression, 125
  feeling, rationality, 101
  management, advice/activities, 127–128
  nonverbal manifestations, impact, 124
  regulation strategies, 127
  release, 126
Empathy, demonstration, 136
Employees
  development, 67, 152
  employers, agreement, 158
  guidance/challenge (signal behavior), 46, 152–153
  implicit contract, 160–161
  listening, 126
  nonadvocacy, scarcity behavior, 45
  supervision/management, 66
  support, 67
  work, perception, 159
Employers, reputation, 159
Employment contract, 158–159
Employment, providing, 41, 55
Encourager, search, 26
Energy
  absolution consumption, reduction, 41, 55
  exuding/conveying, 105–106
  flow, 80–81
  seeking, 121–122
Engels, Friedrich, 39
Enough, definition, 22
Environmental base, importance, 36
Equal Justice Initiative, 90
Evolution, theories, 39
Expectations, implicitness, 160f
Explanation, habits, 27

F

Face time, 82
Facilitation rotation, 92
Failure
  reaction, 67
  systemic failure, 138
Fairness, perception, 159
Fake consensus, impact, 163
Family-wide orientation, 24
Fatalism, sense (creation), 28
Feedback, 67, 121–122, 157
  360-degree feedback, 67–68
  absorption, 137
  giving/receiving, 156
  providing (systems), 60
  seeking/receiving, 156
  work performance feedback, 156
Feyerabend, Paul, 49
Finances, tightness/decline, 66
Financial enterprise, dominance, 41
Financial health, 67
Financial savviness, 106
Finnin, William M., 36
Firewood (carrying), tumpline (usage), 8f
Fluid intelligence, crystallized intelligence (contrast), 111t
Four-day workweek, 69, 73–75
  revisiting, 83
Free enterprise system, 37
Fuller, Richard Buckminster, 69
Functional structures, alignment, 59
Furman, Ezra, 113

G

Gandhi, Mahatma, 48
Garland, Judy, 77
Gender equity, 49
Genesis Grant, 109
Gesell, Arnold, 13f
Gesell Institute
  closure, 14
  offices, 12, 13f

Ghosting, avoidance, 140
Girl Effect, The, 52
Gladwell, Malcolm, 99
Goal alignment, 166
Golden rule, platinum rule (contrast), 142
Gong. *See* Organizational Performance Group
Good local conditions, 136
Good Work Associates (GWA), operation, 14
Grandstanding, 142
Great Mother, 38
Green Village Initiative, 90
Gross, Jenny, 73
Group decision-making, inclusion (spectrum), 165t
Group engagement, spectrum, 163–164
Group expertise, 166
Group think, 163

H
Habitat for Humanity, vision statement, 100
Habitats, restoration, 41, 56
Hackman, Richard, 31
Hancock, Leah, 74
Hand gestures, usage, 124
Hawken, Paul, 39–41
manifesto, 55–56
Health, signs, 146
Herzberg, Frederick, 157
Hierarchy
flattening, 93
sense, 66
Hierarchy of needs (Maslow), 33
Hoarding, 21
Hochschild, Arlie, 123
Hope, exuding/conveying, 105–106
Hopelessness, sense (creation), 28
How-to manual, 95
Humankind, well-being (increase), 40

Humans
breeding, acceleration, 40
relationships (post-scarcity society), 37
Humor, absence, 66
Hybels, Bill, 99
Hygiene factor, 157

I
Ignorance, defense, 142
Immigrants/refugees, hiring (opportunities), 50
Implicit contract, 160–161
Implicit expectations, 160f
Improvement, opportunities, 159
Inclusion methods, 164
Income, reliance, 41, 56
Influence, building, 135
Information
absorption, 137
hoarding (scarcity behavior) (scarcity signal behavior), 46, 47
proactive sharing (signal behavior), 46, 155–156
sharing, 23
Infrastructure solutions, 71
Innovation
bolstering, 73
culture, fostering, 75
encouragement (3M), 108–109
highlighting, 148
Innovators, qualities, 108–109
Insecurity, fostering, 37
Intelligence, conceptualization/ measurement, 110
Intelligence quotient (IQ), 58, 110
Intentionality, 129
Intention/impact, breakdown, 155
Interaction constraint, 166
Internal growth, 59
Internal relationship, change, 8
International Rescue Committee (IRC), service, 9

Interpersonal adeptness, 135–140
  advice/activities, 140
Interpersonal relationship, impact, 11
Interpersonal signaling system, 159
Interview process, 16–17
Intra-system stress, 21

J
J.C. Penney, 142–143
Job functions, delegation, 102
Job security, 159
Johnson, Ron, 142–143
Judger questions, 154f

K
Keating, Steve, 56
Keeble, John, 37–38
Khao-I-Dang refugee camp
  Cambodian refugee, 9f
  Cambodian staff, 12f
  children, classroom attendance, 11
  IRC coordination, 9–10
  office entry sign, 10f
Kickstarter, 74
Knowledge structures, 20
Kozol, Jonathan, 37
Kripalu, 169

L
Lab experiments, participation, 79
Labour, transactional exchange, 159
Leaders
  absence, 27
  aspects, 120
  calmness/evenness, 123–128
  capacity, 32
  discovery, 61
  expertise, 166
  factors, 166
  personal capabilities, impact, 58
  presence, 125–126
  recognition, gaining, 114
  research, usage, 74–75
  structural rethinking, 42

Leadership
  behaviors, range, 19–20
  capability, 56
  characteristic, 56
  difficulty, 118
  ego version, 142
  energy, 67
  focus, change, 119f
  model, absence (explanations),
    19–25
  nonexistence/detriment, 66
  practices/transparency,
    modeling, 114
  role, 118
  roles, phenotype diversity, 110
  situational leadership model,
    164, 166, 168
  styles, taxonomy, 166
  success, 58
  transformational leadership,
    33
  Ulukaya approach, 50
Leading, impact, 146
Learner questions, 154f
Learning, 23
  mindset, 153–154
  opportunities, 159
  questions, usage, 156
Lencioni, Patrick, 63
Leopold, Aldo, 140
Liberating Structures, 82, 169
LinkedIn, vision statement, 100
Listening, importance, 23, 126
Lorimer, Linda, 15
Lousy local conditions, 136
Low emotional/social intelligence
    (scarcity behavior), 45
Lower-level employees,
    empowerment, 67
Lyons, Oren, 48, 101, 141

M
Macrolevers, 69
Malcolm X, 37

Malthus, Thomas Robert (work, significance), 35–36, 42
Managed Heart, The (Hochschild), 123
Management
  circadian rhythm, usage, 77–85
  difficulty, 118
  innovative practices, 93
  micro-management, 15
  open book management, 155
  progression, 119f
  quality, 43, 145
  requirements, 60
  role, 118
Managers
  characteristic, 61
  presence, 125–126
  supportive manager, impact, 159
Managing by walking around (MBWA), 57
Mankind survival, problem (survival), 36
Maraboli, Steve, 117
Market principles, honoring, 41, 55
Market research, usage, 72
Marx, Karl, 39
Maslow (hierarchy of needs), 33
"Mastering Group Facilitation" course, 149
Memes, ideas, 42
Mental models
  basis, 38
  embedded layers, 24f
  examination, 20
  origin, 21
  purposes, 20
  requirement, 146
Meta-competencies, 43, 99–100, 113, 117, 145
Microlevers, 7, 88
  advice/activities, 93
Micro-management, 15
Microsoft Japan, 74

Mind chatter, 131–132
Mindful meditation, usage, 127
Minimum specifications, 82
Misfortune, optimists (perspective), 26
Mission
  focus, 50
  statement, development/ enhancement, 59
Mistakes
  allowance, 125
  inevitability, 125
  learning, 156
Mistrust (scarcity behavior), 46
Money, energy transfer, 106
Monkey mind, 131–133
Mood, nonverbal manifestations (impact), 124
Moral compass, strength, 141
Moral dilemma, advice (seeking), 142
Morale, importance, 67
Morality, 140–142
  advice/activities, 141–142
  relativism, 141
Morality of Scarcity, The (Finnin/ Smith), 36
Moral person, indicators, 141
Mother Theresa, 87
Moveable furniture, usage, 79f
Multiple intelligences, 110

N

Narration, characteristic, 134
Natural resource
  absolute consumption, reduction, 41, 55
  scarcity, problem, 35–36
Needs, discussion (avoidance), 137
Niels Diffrient, 75
Nonbudget resources, 162
Non-unionized environment, 6–7
Nonverbal cues, adjustment, 124
Nonverbal signals, impact, 140

O

Objectives (obtaining), emotions (display), 126
Obstacles, overcoming, 32
Ogalala Aquifer, drying, 40
Omega Institute, 169
Open book management, 155
OPG Inspire Podcast, 169
Opinion, seeking, 121–122
Optimism, 25–30
  impact, 26
  indication, 28
  leaders, absence, 27
Organizational boundaries, maintenance, 158–162
Organizational citizens, creation, 103
Organizational development (OD), 59–60
  research/benchmarking, 14
Organizational health, 63
  improvement, 65
Organizational health measure (OHM), 65
  attributes, 66–67
Organizational life, voting (avoidance), 164
Organizational Performance Group (OPG), 3, 49
  annual donation, 89–90
  charrette, 70–73
    results, 73f
  check-ins, 91–92, 126
  collective memory, 90–91
  community wall, 90
  conference room (Aquarium), 77f
    clients, presence, 78f
    moveable furniture, usage, 79f
  creation, 17
  facilitation rotation, 92
  Friday meetings, ban, 84
  gallery, 91f
  good news gong, 88, 89f
  ideal world, imagining, 93
  lab notes, usage, 83

portfolio, 96
public agenda, 90
results, 84–85
"share your travels" shelves, 92f
snow globes, usage, 91–92
staff members
  circadian rhythm, 80f
  discussions, 83–84
standards, 82, 84
team investment, 83
turnover rate, 66
"who are you outside of work" gallery, 91f
Organizations
  ecosystem, 47
  energy/enthusiasm, generation, 103
  improvement, 30, 36, 59–60
  leadership, nonexistence/detriment, 66
  management
    quality, 60–62
    requirements, 57
  mission statement, development/enhancement, 59
  ongoing operations, improvement, 60
  productive exercises, 75
Outcomes, faith, 23

P

Pandemic
  impact, 85
  nourishment, supply, 50
Panos, Tony, 27, 122, 126, 154
Paradigm shift, 74
Pathologization, avoidance, 104–105
Pay, perceived fairness, 159
Pedal-operated poster rolling machine, 6f
People
  perception, importance, 57
  responsibility/accountability, 66
Pepper, John, 17
Perfection, attempt, 59

Perks and Benefits package, perceived fairness, 159
Permanence, 27
Perpetual Guardian, 74–75
Personal boundaries, 161f
Personal capabilities, 58
Personality fit, problem, 11
Personalization (optimism/pessimism indication), 28
Personal property lines, 161f
Personal satisfaction, 102
Personal vision
  creation, 102
  sample, 103f
Pervasiveness, 27–28
Pessimism, indication, 28–29
Pessimist, sign, 28
Phenotypes, diversity, 110
Physically visibility, 114
Picket lines, reappearance, 7
Piercy, Marge, 29
Planet, People, Profit, and Purpose (4 Ps), results, 490
Planned improvements, making, 59
Platinum rule, golden rule (contrast), 142
Policies/procedures, development (assistance), 60
Population growth, dynamics, 35–36
Porter, Michael, 31
Position, power, 120
Positive abundance mental model, 27
Positive thinking, impact, 26
Post-scarcity, meaning, 37
Posture, attention, 124
Power
  abuse (scarcity behavior) (scarcity signal behavior), 46, 47
  appropriate usage, 67
Practice, theory (relationship), 39f
Praise, giving, 23
Pre-charrette questionnaire, 72
Prezi, vision statement, 100

Primary greatness, 31
Priorities, sense, 122
Problem solving
  methods, 108–109
  signal behavior, 46
Problems, origination, 138
Process redesign, impact, 148–149
Production, means, 38
Productivity
  focus, 4
  importance, 66
  increase, 74, 130
Profits
  maximization, 40
  sharing, 32
Progress, 30, 36
Promotion
  example, 5–6
  opportunities, 159
  usage, 66
Protection, 157–162
  advice/activities, 162
  management skill, 62
Psyche (post-scarcity society), 37
Psychological boundaries, maintenance, 158–162
Psychological contract, 158–159
  aspects, 159
  breakdown, 160
Psychological contracting, 158–159
Psychosynthesis, 134
Public agenda, 90
Purpose, knowledge, 149

R

"Radically Transformative Indicators," 104
Rayford, Brett, 58
Ray, Paul, 42
Recognition, sharing, 32
Reflection/affect, 121–135
  advice/activities, 135
Resource-abundant systems, 21–22

Resources
  scarcity, 36–37
  seeking, 157–158
Resource-scarce systems, 21–22
Response, consideration, 126
Responsibility, sharing, 32
Revenue shortfalls, 108
Reward systems, creation, 60
Reynolds, Jock, 104
Richard, Alison, 15
Risk, involvement, 110
Roche, Robert, 69

S

Scarcity
  behaviors, 31–32, 43, 45–46
  bosses, interaction (difficulty), 47
  fear, decrease, 21
  mentality, 22, 31–32
    manifestation, 22
    source, 32
  mental model, 21, 22
  mind-set, 32
  mirroring, 30
  orientation, 21–23
  reaction, 25
  signal behaviors, 46–47
Scarcity-abundance spectrum, 21
Scarcity-mentality leadership, 23
Schaef, Anne Wilson, 142
Seed capital (3M structure/
    system), 109
Self-actuation, usage, 41, 55
Self-awareness, 43, 58–59,
    117, 119–120
  elevation, 47
  inner compass, 58
Self-care, time management
    (relationship), 129–130
Self-criticism, impact, 133
Self-efficacy, 59
Self-employment, reasons, 3
Self-interested individuals,
    achievements, 38

Self-knowledge, signs, 122
Self-worth, 133
Seligman, Martin, 26–29
Sexual harassment, 51
Sharing, increase, 21
Sherpas, work, 8–9
Showry, K. Mansas, 58
Signal behaviors, 46
  scarcity signal behaviors, 46–47
Signaling
  impact, 88
  interpersonal signaling system, 159
Silent Spring (Carson), 36
Situational factors, 166
Situational leadership model,
    164, 166, 168
Skepticism, creation, 163
Skills
  development, 103
  learning, 58
Skills of Encouragement, The, 26
Smith, Gerald A., 36
Snow globes, usage, 91–92
Social construction, problem, 110
Social relations, 37
Soft skills, rating, 58
Solutions, implementation, 38
Soros, George, 38
Southwest Airlines, vision
    statement, 100
Spaces, design, 76
Spheres of influence, 132f
Spheres of influence thinking, 132
Staff members
  cattiness/pettiness, presence, 66
  circadian rhythm, 80f
  discussions, data (insights), 83–84
  engagement, 76
  guiding principles, 84
  protection, 157–158
  recruitment, difficulty, 140
  resources, obtaining, 157–158
Stange, Jocelyn, 125
Status, determination, 133

Steinbock, Dan, 9, 152
Strategic plan, creation, 59
Strategic planning, 102
    OPG definition, 103
    process, 103–104
    texts, 31
Strategy work, 71
Stress
    handling, 127
    intra-system stress, 21
Substandard performance, toleration
        (scarcity behavior), 45
Successes, celebration (scarcity
        behavior), 45
Supportive manager, impact, 159
Suspiciousness (scarcity behavior), 46
Sustainability, 35
    concept, 36
    exceeding, actions, 41, 56
    practice/theory, relationship, 39
    theory, development, 39
Symbiotic relationship, 11
System embeddedness, 138f
Systemic failure, 138
System-wide solutions, 138–139

T

Taos Institute, 169
Team
    accomplishment, celebration, 153
    competence, 166
    coordination/empowerment, 153
    Drexler-Sibbet team performance
        model, 147f
    dynamics, awareness, 11
    empowerment, 125
    OPG investment, 83
    success, roles (signal behavior), 46
    success, roles (understanding/
        articulating), 147–151
    work, recognition (gaining), 114
Team building, 146–153
    advice/activities, 153
    management skill, 61

    model, 149–150
    opportunities, 147–151
        signal behavior, 46
Teamwork, camaraderie, 66
Technical expertise, 109–110
Technical skills, 58
*Thinking Today as if Tomorrow
        Mattered* (Adams), 41
Thirty Percent Rule, 108–109
Time-driven models, 166
Time, importance, 166
Time management, 128–135
    self-care, relationship, 129–130
Tiredness, feeling (rationality), 101
"To Be of Use" (Piercy), 29–30
Trait-based leaders, characteristics,
        34
Trait-based leadership, 33
Transformational leadership, 33
Transformational leaders, vision/
        inspiration, 34
Trends, research, 72
Triangulation, occurrence, 11
Trust, culture (building), 125
Trustworthiness, 141
Turnover rate, 66

U

Ulukaya, Hamdi, 49–50, 50f
Unanimity, existence, 164
Unilever, 74
Unions, appearance, 7
United Nations High Commissioner
        for Refugees (UNHCR)
        representatives, impact, 10
Upside of Anger, The (film), 124
Urgency, sense (reduction), 150

V

Vallone, Peter, 14–17
Value, manifestation, 88
Vaughan, Sarah, 29–30
Venture formation (3M structure/
        system), 109

Visibility, 43, 56–57, 113
  advice/activities, 115
  competency, 114
  example, 114
  qualities, 114
Vision
  absence (scarcity behavior), 46
  communication, 100–102
  manifestation, 88
  personal vision, creation, 102,
    102f
  statements, examples, 100
Visioning, 43, 48–56, 99, 100–106
  advice/activities, 106
  competencies, 100
Voice, relentlessness/pain, 133–134
Voting, avoidance, 164
Vroom, Victor, 163
  decision-making methods, 167f
  situational leadership model,
    164, 166, 168

W

Walled-off workstations/spaces,
  usage, 77
Way of life, rewards, 41
Wealth, generation, 37
What-if scenarios, creation, 132
Whole systems, thinking, 23

Wilber, Ken, 38, 42
Willis, Daniel, 70
Winkler, Henry (Fonzi photo), 5f
Wolfe Herd, Whitney, 51–52, 52f
Women
  marginalization, 136
  work, undervaluation, 55
Words, flow, 33
Work
  choice, 137
  environment, creation, 78–79
  experience, impact, 17
  intangible benefits,
    requirement, 102
  performance feedback, 156
Workforce, environment, 7
Work/home life intersection, 102
Work-life balance, 130
Working environment, assessment, 60
Work-life balance, nonencourage-
  ment (scarcity behavior), 45
Workplace
  humanity, return, 126
  quality, intuition (usage), 66
Workspace design, 69, 75–77
Wright, Gretchen, 69
Written employment contract,
  usage, 158
Written plan, production, 103